# Building Web Apps with Ember.js

*Jesse Cravens and Thomas Q Brady*

Beijing · Cambridge · Farnham · Köln · Sebastopol · Tokyo

**Building Web Apps with Ember.js**

by Jesse Cravens and Thomas Q Brady

Printed in the United States of America.

Published by O'Reilly Media, Inc. , 1005 Gravenstein Highway North, Sebastopol, CA 95472.

O'Reilly books may be purchased for educational, business, or sales promotional use. Online editions are also available for most titles (*http://my.safaribooksonline.com* (*http://my.safaribooksonline.com/?por tal=oreilly*)). For more information, contact our corporate/institutional sales department: 800-998-9938 or corporate@oreilly.com.

| | |
|---|---|
| **Editors:** Simon St. Laurent and Brian MacDonald | **Indexer:** Judy McConville |
| **Production Editor:** Kara Ebrahim | **Interior Designer:** David Futato |
| **Copyeditor:** Jasmine Kwityn | **Cover Designer:** Ellie Volckhausen |
| **Proofreader:** Amanda Kersey | **Illustrator:** Rebecca Demarest |

July 2014:       First Edition

**Revision History for the First Edition**
2014-07-07:    First Release

See *http://oreilly.com/catalog/errata.csp?isbn=9781449370923* for release details.

978-1-449-37092-3

[LSI]

# Table of Contents

# Preface

## Building Web Apps with Ember.js

Welcome to *Building Web Apps with Ember.js*! This book is largely about building production-capable, browser-based appplicatons. Some might call these single-page apps while others say HTML5 apps, client MVC apps, or rich Internet apps; but in the end, these types of applications are one and the same: the web browser is the application platform, and the server provides remote service endpoints. After years of writing and using many of the solutions available to manage complex applications of this type, we have settled on Ember.js as our primary toolset. In this book, we will attempt to both teach you what we know about Ember, and, along the way, demonstrate for you why it has become our primary toolset for building web applications.

In 2005, I (Jesse) discovered JavaScript and the `XMLHttpRequest` object while working at a digital agency that deployed .NET and Drupal applications with rich, Flash and web frontends. At the time, JavaScript was a disrespected "toy" language used to *sprinkle* functionality onto the top of traditional web applications. Ironically, much of the JavaScript work I did then involved using flashvars to create a bridge between PHP and browser-based Flash applications.

But, at the time, Flash frontends were a necessary evil. Browsers were largely incapable of supporting rich, interactive experiences, and respectable JavaScript libraries like MooTools, YUI, and Dojo were only beginning to mature.

As I began taking additional risks by using more and more JavaScript in my applications, I started to find other like-minded developers that also believed that browsers would evolve and that JavaScript was more than just a toy language. We believed JavaScript was a full-featured, object-oriented, professional language that was capable of being used to build high-performing production applications. A strong community began to evolve, fueled largely by pioneers like Douglass Crockford, John Resig, Paul Irish, and Christian Heilmann to name a few, and eventually *frontend developer* became a professional job class in many organizations.

In 2007, I took my JavaScript skills to the enterprise. I was hired to begin building a complex, rich Internet application within an enterprise J2EE stack. This introduced me to many of the most common challenges presented by large-scale development: lack of JavaScript and frontend expertise, server-centric web legacy, complex cross-browser and mobile-web fragmentation compatibility requirements, and lack of provisioned desktop and development tooling for frontend developers, just to name a few. Being faced with all these limitations was some of the most challenging work of my career—not to mention overcoming the naysayers that didn't want to see the end of safe, traditional web applications.

Over the next couple of years, I focused solely on implementing and deploying a solution that was in many ways before its time. Many of the tools that are available today were nascent, or nonexistent at the time, including client MV* libraries, client-side routing and object relational mappers (ORMs), JavaScript templates, JavaScript promises, async flow control libraries, and web components. Nevertheless, my team and I dreamed up and implemented custom solutions within the parameters of the project timelines and requirements. Overall it was a success, and our client MVC framework still remains in production today.

Since 2009, I have worked on numerous applications using Backbone, Angular, and Ember. But today, I often recommend Ember.js to the clients I work with. This is primarily due to the fact that the conventions support well-known web application development patterns that I have custom written or pieced together from multiple open source libraries. Here, are the high level concepts that, in my opinion, make Ember so valuable:

- Ember's object model supports a classic and well understood, object-oriented pattern of class inheritance through extend, object initialization, getters and setters, and class monkey patching.

- Ember models, controllers, and components extend the `Object` class, which ensures that these objects inherit Ember's powerful default data binding.

- The router supports complex nesting for URL-driven applications that manage application state in a conventional way that can be understood by those with web-server-routing backgrounds.

- Recently, build, workflow, and testing tools in Ember have matured and become intuitive.

- Ember's only dependencies are on jQuery and Handlebars.js, two very well-known and documented libraries.

- Finally, the community is vibrant, passionate, and extremely active.

In late 2012 and 2013, Thomas Brady and I found ourselves working on numerous ambitious web UIs in our work at frog design (*http://www.frogdesign.com/*). Despite the nascency of the framework at the time, we felt Ember was the right tool for the job. We believed in the direction the framework was heading and in the community of talented developers behind it. At times it was frustrating, but in the end, I find myself saying all the time, "Can you imagine what it would take to do this in another framework?"

# More Than Just "Getting Started"

If you are picking up this book, we assume you have interest in building full-stack, single-page applications. In other words, we assume that you would not only like to architect and build a fully functional, browser-based application, but also connect it to a backend. That being said, this book covers all aspects of building applications with Ember. So, in addition to providing you with a complete overview of the HTML and JavaScript necessary to write on the frontend, we also include an implicit project timeline via the structure and order of the chapters, development workflow and tooling, and example backend technologies that help with getting the remotely persisted data in a format that Ember and Ember Data can easily work with.

You may be asking why we are covering all these aspects of Ember.js development. Why not just build a frontend Ember app?

Well, before we lose you, rest assured we will cover all the basics you need in Chapter 1 and Chapter 2. The approach we take in the remainder of the book will hopefully provide more value and context. We feel there are numerous example applications that already provide the necessary beginner information. These applications are very valuable, as they provide the basics and are fantastic starting points. But when you try to meet the needs of a more complex application within the context of delivering a production product, many development teams get stuck not knowing where to start, which tools to use in development, and which backend technologies should be chosen to persist data.

# Navigating This Book

So, first and foremost, the demo application we will develop throughout the book intentionally covers many of the areas of development not included in most of the *getting started* applications. We also try to do this without creating an application that is too complicated so that we don't lose the beginner or the developer that hasn't yet been exposed to single-page application development in general.

Throughout the book, we provide sidebars for some of the more challenging and less documented aspects of Ember development, such as application initializers, active generation, promises, and debugging.

Establishing a pro workflow for your project can be a decision nightmare. Early on in Chapter 3, we get this out of the way and cover most of the major tooling options so that you'll have a head start in getting you and your team set up for success.

In Chapter 4, we begin working with HTML, building templates using Handlebars.js, and extending Handlebars to create our own Handlebars helpers. The fact that we can begin with HTML is an important nuance to Ember development that works well within a project workflow that makes minimizing duplication of efforts a high priority.

Then in Chapter 5, we dive into the router, and begin to structure the various states of our application and reflect those states in our URLs. Again, the fact that we are doing this now is an important aspect to take notice of. We are prototyping, but our code will very likely survive the transition to production.

Chapter 6 fills in the rest of the blanks, introducing controllers, data binding, and views.

It is often advantageous to cache your data in client-side data stores to optimize the application so that it makes as few round trips to the server as possible. There are a number of client-side persistence solutions available. Chapter 7 covers models and Ember Data, the most *official* data persistence solution for Ember.

It has also been our experience that getting the backend talking to the frontend, without project churn, is one of the most difficult aspects of delivering a project. In Chapter 8, we begin building service layers that will connect your remote persistence layer to Ember's client-side data store. Most importantly, we will do it in a developer-friendly way through abstractions, known as adapters, to ensure efficient, project-phase transitions.

Chapter 9 covers the basics of Ember components, a standardized (Web Components) approach to building functionality in a modular way, and also integration with the third-party visualization library, D3.js.

And finally, we cover both integration and unit testing best practices in Chapter 10.

# Conventions Used in This Book

The following typographical conventions are used in this book:

*Italic*
> Indicates new terms, URLs, email addresses, filenames, and file extensions.

`Constant width`
> Used for program listings, as well as within paragraphs to refer to program elements such as variable or function names, databases, data types, environment variables, statements, and keywords.

**Constant width bold**

Shows commands or other text that should be typed literally by the user.

*Constant width italic*

Shows text that should be replaced with user-supplied values or by values determined by context.

 This icon signifies a tip, suggestion, or general note.

 This icon indicates a warning or caution.

# Using Code Examples

Supplemental material (code examples, exercises, etc.) is available for download at *https://github.com/emberjsbook*.

This book is here to help you get your job done. In general, if example code is offered with this book, you may use it in your programs and documentation. You do not need to contact us for permission unless you're reproducing a significant portion of the code. For example, writing a program that uses several chunks of code from this book does not require permission. Selling or distributing a CD-ROM of examples from O'Reilly books does require permission. Answering a question by citing this book and quoting example code does not require permission. Incorporating a significant amount of example code from this book into your product's documentation does require permission.

We appreciate, but do not require, attribution. An attribution usually includes the title, author, publisher, and ISBN. For example: *"Building Web Apps with Ember.js* by Jesse Cravens and Thomas Q Brady (O'Reilly). Copyright 2014 Jesse Cravens and Thomas Q Brady, 978-1-4493-7092-3."

If you feel your use of code examples falls outside fair use or the permission given above, feel free to contact us at *permissions@oreilly.com*.

# Safari® Books Online

 *Safari Books Online* is an on-demand digital library that delivers expert content in both book and video form from the world's leading authors in technology and business.

Technology professionals, software developers, web designers, and business and creative professionals use Safari Books Online as their primary resource for research, problem solving, learning, and certification training.

Safari Books Online offers a range of product mixes and pricing programs for organizations, government agencies, and individuals. Subscribers have access to thousands of books, training videos, and prepublication manuscripts in one fully searchable database from publishers like O'Reilly Media, Prentice Hall Professional, Addison-Wesley Professional, Microsoft Press, Sams, Que, Peachpit Press, Focal Press, Cisco Press, John Wiley & Sons, Syngress, Morgan Kaufmann, IBM Redbooks, Packt, Adobe Press, FT Press, Apress, Manning, New Riders, McGraw-Hill, Jones & Bartlett, Course Technology, and dozens more. For more information about Safari Books Online, please visit us online.

# How to Contact Us

Please address comments and questions concerning this book to the publisher:

O'Reilly Media, Inc.
1005 Gravenstein Highway North
Sebastopol, CA 95472
800-998-9938 (in the United States or Canada)
707-829-0515 (international or local)
707-829-0104 (fax)

We have a web page for this book, where we list errata, examples, and any additional information. You can access this page at *http://bit.ly/bwa-emberjs*.

To comment or ask technical questions about this book, send email to *bookquestions@oreilly.com*.

For more information about our books, courses, conferences, and news, see our website at *http://www.oreilly.com*.

Find us on Facebook: *http://facebook.com/oreilly*

Follow us on Twitter: *http://twitter.com/oreillymedia*

Watch us on YouTube: *http://www.youtube.com/oreillymedia*

## Acknowledgments

Many thanks for all the hard work provided by numerous individuals within the Ember community and of course, the Ember core team. The momentum and change within the community has created enormous challenges in building projects for clients and keeping the information in this book up to date. But it is all worth it when an API becomes more intuitive or a new feature is merged into core. Thanks for responding to our stack overflows and IRC questions and supporting the creation of this book.

Special thanks to all of our reviewers and editors at O'Reilly, and to technical reviewer Adam Luikart.

And finally, thanks to our wives and families for supporting us throughout the authoring process.

# CHAPTER 1

# Introducing Ember.js and Ambitious Web Applications

These days, we web developers have it relatively easy. No, we're not just celebrating the consensus that Internet Explorer 6 need no longer be fully supported—OK, yes, we're also doing that. You see, in our day, we had to reinvent the wheel a lot. At the start of any given project, you would go scouring through previous projects for bits and pieces of JavaScript you'd written or borrowed that did things like iron out API differences between browsers, set up utility functions you'd grown accustomed to, and even generate HTML bits in reusable ways.

It happened so much that it felt less like reinventing the wheel and more like running inside a hamster wheel. We have a feeling that's why Ember (hereafter referred to that way, without the ".js") uses that cute little hamster as its mascot. Ember jumps into the wheel for you, freeing you to concentrate on what's new and interesting about *your particular* project. We have it easy these days because we have our pick of dozens of well-designed toolchains, libraries, frameworks, and the like that offer such conveniences, but this book is about why Ember is particularly well suited to help you build ambitious web applications.

Ember won't be useful to you, let alone make any sense to you, without understanding some of the underlying technologies and concepts it builds upon, as well as the problems it hopes to solve, so let's dissect some of those first.

## What Is an "Ambitious Web Application"?

Ember came to be as a successor—perhaps more a "spiritual cousin"—to the web-application framework SproutCore, a framework you've quite likely encountered on the Web, knowingly or otherwise.   If you've used any of Apple's iCloud (formerly

MobileMe) applications to check your email, locate and even remotely disable your phone with "Find My Phone," or, most recently, create Pages, Numbers, or Keynote documents on the Web, you've used SproutCore. These are great examples of ambitious web applications: ones that look and act like desktop applications, but happen to be delivered via web technologies.

Such applications differ from much of web development in several important ways.

## Ambitious Web Applications Are Not Documents

We tend to think that any sentence that starts with, "When Tim Berners-Lee" can be safely ignored, unless written by Sir Berners-Lee, but this time you'll just have to trust us. When Sir Tim Berners-Lee created the World Wide Web, he was pretty clear about the use case he was building for. The backbone of his invention was the Hypertext Transport Protocol (HTTP). He was creating a better way to share documents. In his own words (*http://www.achievement.org/autodoc/page/ber1int-1*), he was "thinking about all the documentation systems out there as being possibly part of a larger imaginary documentation system." This powerful technology allowed a browser to turn a URL, provided by the user, into a unique address to a server, which could be located anywhere in the world, and even to a specific document on that server, which could then be retrieved and rendered for the user. Browsing a site like Wikipedia is a canonical example of this model. When you click a link on a Wikipedia page or search for an entry on the site, the browser sends a request to load a new document—from a new URL. The entire page is replaced with the new content, and the URL shown to the user in the address bar changes. Although this is still a remarkable feat, it bears little resemblance to the expectations of a modern "web application." In the years since the birth of the Web, we've come to expect a lot from desktop applications, from real-time data manipulations to eye-catching renderings and animations. In recent years, we've come to expect "web applications" to be no different.

## Ambitious Web Applications Are Stateful

By design, the building blocks of the Web are stateless. "State," for our purposes anyway, refers to data that changes and must be persisted in your application. For instance, if your user has checked a checkbox in your web form, you don't want to uncheck that checkbox accidentally, just because you've forgotten. You want to remember that the state in which you found the checkbox last was "checked," and that it should stay that way until a legitimate reason for it to change—the user clicks it again, or some logical scenario requires it be toggled or unchecked—comes along. Since HTTP is a stateless protocol, there's nothing being passed back and forth between your browser and the server that describe this sort of state data. If you're simply navigating from document to document, no state is necessary. If you're building an application, however, you need to know things such as:

- Is this user logged in?
- Has this order been placed?
- Has this message been sent?

Over the years, web developers have figured out a number of hacks for persisting state across sessions, using protocols that weren't designed to enable such a thing. We've used URL-encoded state variables, cookies, and the like to keep track of what the user has done and is doing across multiple HTTP requests.

Those of us old enough to have used the Web in those days remember the pain of typing in a long expense report, email, blog post, or some more important document, only to have it disappear into the ether(net) when one of these state-persistence hacks failed. Until we filled this gap in the Web's feature set, it would remain a document-delivery platform. When we'd truly solved this problem, the Web became an application platform. The solution to this problem was the XMLHTTPRequest, or XHR, a nigh-magical new capability that allowed your application logic to request data from or send data to the server without itself being unloaded and reloaded.

Microsoft gets a lot of flak from the web-development community, mostly for the sins visited on the world in the form of Internet Explorer versions previous to 8. To be sure, there were some serious oversights in those software releases. However, Microsoft is responsible, at least in part, for several of the Web's biggest advancements. Internet Explorer 5.0 for the Macintosh was the first browser to fully support CSS (*http://bit.ly/1qR9fPU*), for instance. It was also Microsoft that invented the XHR (*http://bit.ly/1qR9iLA*).

The XHR abstracts the very soul of the browser; it allows JavaScript to make an HTTP request, just as the browser did historically, and deal directly with the response. This puts JavaScript—thereby, the JavaScript *developer*, not the browser itself —in control of the user experience. The user can enter a URL, such as *http://mail.google.com*, into the browser's address bar, and the browser will load the Gmail application. From then on, the Gmail application's JavaScript code is able to make additional HTTP requests to acquire more data—individual email documents, attachments, updated copies of the user's address book, and gobs more—without reloading the page. If you don't need to reload the page, it's not necessary to jump through as many hoops to preserve state. Much has been written about how this made the Web more responsive, how it made web applications look and act more like desktop software. Gmail and Google Maps dazzled us with their desktop-grade experience and performance. Crucially, though, the XHR had the subtle effect of gaining our trust in the Web as a platform for application delivery.

With XHR, when a user hits "send" in an email application, for instance, the application can fire off a request to deliver the email data to the server. If this XHR fails, the page and all its data—including the email the user has written—remain on the page and in memory. The application can simply try again to deliver the data. This, in our opinion, fundamentally changed the Web. In combination with its newfound performance, this reliability made the Web a "real" application platform.

The trouble, then, became managing all the state that was not being flushed with regular page reloads.

## Ambitious Web Applications Are Long-Lived

Modern web applications are now *long-lived*, meaning the application could be open in a browser instance for hours at a time without reloading the page. The upside, as we've celebrated, is that you can load gobs of additional data from the server without having to reload your application every time. The downside is that you now have to manage those gobs of data. If you simply keep adding data without releasing any of it, you will fill up your RAM in short order, locking up the browser and showing your user a "busy" cursor.

Ember, through features and through conventions, helps you take advantage of long-lived application development while avoiding memory leaks. Ember's view management automatically cleans up unused variables and bindings for you as views are shown and hidden. Ember's conventions for navigating from one view to another also encourage you to pass objects from one to another, saving you the trip to the server to reload data for a particular view, if it has already been loaded, and saving you from inadvertently having two or more copies of the same object in memory.

And potential memory leaks aren't the only challenge. The kind of application that sticks around for several hours won't likely all fit within a jQuery `ready` callback. Without some smart structure to your codebase, adding and maintaining features that could be used at any time and repeatedly can become quite difficult.

### What's in a Name?

So, imagine you're a web developer in 2005, and you've decided you want to use XHR to completely overhaul the web-based software you develop at work. You're going to be in a lot of meetings with lots of people who would not describe themselves as tech savvy, attempting to convince them to allow you to extend deadlines, hire more developers, and redesign user interfaces because of this new feature available to you. You click your presentation remote, and a slide appears in front of the room that says, "Extensible Markup Language (XML) Hypertext Transport Protocol (HTTP) Request, or XHR." OK, it actually takes two slides, but you never get to the second slide because there are too many questions, and you get interrupted too many times by stakeholders trying to sound smart by yelling their own explanations of how "the Internet is a series of tubes" over you.

If you were Jesse James Garrett, this didn't happen to you, because you instead came up with a catchy, clever explanation of the technology and wrote an article entitled "Ajax: A New Approach to Web Applications" (*http://bit.ly/1oNW3Lf*). "Ajax" stands for "Asynchronous JavaScript and XML," and we'll let you do your own research as to what it means and has meant to the Web. For the purposes of this book, it was the sexy marketing name for XHR and what it did for statefulness in web applications.

XML, by the way, has started appearing in those "Where are they now?" segments in the web-application gossip magazines. For our purposes, it has very nearly been obviated by JSON—JavaScript Object Notation, a data format not unlike XML, but written in a JavaScript-friendly format.

You may have heard the term "single-page application" or seen it abbreviated "SPA." This transitional term (and misnomer—these applications almost always involve numerous "pages") is another way of describing applications that don't reload the entire page for most or all interactions. This term arose because Ajax is not the only way to accomplish this sort of user experience. These days there are a number of ways to get additional data after an initial page load, from WebSockets to local storage.

## Ambitious Web Applications Have Architecture

Now that we have these long-lived pages persisting all of this state data, we're going to need some organization and planning. If the code that enables the user to write an email is living on the same page as the code to allow the user to delete an email, we have to ensure that the right bit of code is executing so we don't delete an email we intend to send. We want to make sure the right data is being accessed—we don't want the code that sends the body of an email to accidentally send the user's address book instead. And if we create a great scrolling list feature for our inbox, we don't want to have to do all that work again for our sent items, junk mail, and favorites lists.

In the late 1970s, architects began thinking about common design challenges and their solutions as reusable *patterns*. Rather than starting every project with a blank slate and independently arriving at the conclusion that *this* doctor's office was going to need a large room with lots of seating where patients could wait until the doctor was ready to see them, they identified *design patterns*, such as the "waiting room," an abstract concept that could be implemented whenever useful. You could then have a name for the phenomenon and ask questions such as, "Do we really need a waiting room for this build?" You could also better define the concept itself: "You can't have a waiting room without places to sit."

### Model-view-"whatever-you-want-to-call-it"

A few years later, information architects realized the same approach could be useful in software architecture. We software architects were already employing a similar, if more abstract approach with . For software architecture, design patterns could give us a middle ground—between *object* and *implementation*—to talk about common feature sets and requirements. One of the more popular patterns to come out of this movement was the , which describes:

- A *model*, in the sense of a mathematical model, that describes a set of domain-specific data. An application can, and likely does, include multiple models. A user model, for instance, would include attributes describing users, such as their names, dates of birth, permissions, and so on.

- A *view*, which is the face of the application, the representation of the model data and features the application offers for interacting with that data. Most often in software this is a graphical user interface (GUI) with text, images, and widgets, such as buttons, dropdowns, and form fields.

- A *controller*, which is the home of the application logic and can access the model, populates the view with data retrieved from the model and responds to interaction events instigated by the user and relayed by the view, in turn manipulating the data in the model and controlling which of potentially multiple views is in use.

This pattern has seen extraordinary success in desktop software and server-side architectures in the last 30 years, but it's a relatively new concept for web developers. A few years ago, a server-side engineer friend of ours asked, "Why are client-side developers talking about MVC so much all of a sudden? What do they care? They *are* the view!"

There are myriad flavors and interpretations of MVC, many of which take issue with the term "controller." For that reason, you may see it abbreviated MV* so as to include patterns that replace the "controller" with "routers," "view controllers," and other concepts.

Separating your code into packages dedicated to models, views, and controllers is not magic. It's simply a way to ensure that you're separating concerns, encapsulating functionality and data into discrete objects with a singular, modular purpose, the way a good object-oriented programmer should. It's also a conventional organization. If you know that someone employed the MVC pattern in a project, you know where to go looking for feature implementations. It makes it easier to debug and maintain someone else's code, or even your own.

---

## What's OOP?

Object-oriented programming (OOP) itself is not a concept that's necessarily familiar to all web developers. Although its scope is too broad to attempt to cover it here, there have been many, many books written on the topic. For a very friendly, non-programming-language-specific approach, try *Karel++* (Wiley). You can read the first

---

couple chapters online (*http://csis.pace.edu/~bergin/karel.html*) and follow a link to purchasing options if you like it. Our publisher, O'Reilly, is the definitive source for all things programming, and has dozens of books tackling OOP concepts in the abstract, or for whatever language you happen to be using. In particular, we recommend *JavaScript: The Good Parts* and *Learning JavaScript Design Patterns*.

# What Is Ember.js?

Ah, yes. It's been a few pages since we even mentioned Ember, hasn't it? As we established earlier, Ember is a cousin to SproutCore, a project which was, and is, an attempt to create a desktop-class software development kit (SDK) for the web platform.

JavaScript's object-oriented model is pretty different from that of C++, Java, and other, more traditional interpretations. JavaScript employs a prototype model, a more dynamic, expressive method of implementing inheritance that seems to have a polarizing effect on developers. Some love it. Some hate it. Many, though, are confused by it or even unaware of it.

One of the major features of SproutCore 1.0 was a bolted-on object inheritance system that more closely resembled that of C++ or Java, offering object extension and more traditional class definitions. Where Ember and SproutCore differ most is that SproutCore also included a library of pre-built UI widgets, as many SDKs do. Just as an Objective-C developer can drop in a Cocoa dropdown widget rather than creating such a thing from scratch, SproutCore developers can drop in ready-made interface widgets with pre-built styling, functionality, and documentation. Ember forgoes including such a library in favor of encouraging you, the developer, to use the native library of your platform: HTML, JavaScript, and CSS.

In short, Ember.js is, as they put front and center on *emberjs.com*, "a framework for creating ambitious web applications." It builds on jQuery, the ubiquitous JavaScript framework that smoothes out browser inconsistencies and adds a plethora of utility functions to JavaScript, and Handlebars, a library that offers HTML templating in JavaScript. Beyond the technology involved, Ember is a set of conventions for building robust, testable performant software. These conventions include everything from "here's where this kind of code should be found within the project" to "here's how you should name your classes."

# Why Choose Ember?

Ember is not the only solution, and it's not for everyone. The concept of "convention over configuration" is a polarizing one in developer communities. If you like convention (if you're a Ruby on Rails fan, for instance), you'll probably love Ember. If you prefer to pare down your application stack and finely tune each piece, you may still enjoy Ember. Ember doesn't prevent you from this kind of configuration, though it can make some of it more cumbersome than you might like.

Here are the main selling points of Ember:

- Easy, fast, two-way data binding
- What they call "developer ergonomics" (more on this in the next section)
- Ember Data, which provides lots of ORM features and adapts to and abstracts away nearly any backend
- Built-in URL/history management that's tied to data and state automatically
- Views built in HTML

That last bullet might not seem like a big deal, but if you've built an application in a framework that declares its views in JavaScript, rather than HTML, you can probably appreciate the difference. Declaring tag names, class names, inner text values, and other attributes in JavaScript is verbose, difficult to read, and requires someone who can "speak" JavaScript to write. Templates written in HTML can be created and edited by designers who know just enough HTML to be dangerous.

## Developer Ergonomics?

You'll see this phrase a lot in the documentation at *emberjs.com*: "Because this pattern is so common, it is the default for…" This indicates you don't even need to type the code it's describing; Ember will "just work" without it, employing the default behavior as though you'd specified it. As we'll see in the next chapter, you can invoke a default route and a default controller just by instantiating an Ember application. With a single line of JavaScript (before minifying, *wisenheimer*) and a Handlebars template, Ember will fill in all the gaps with default objects, and you end up with a complete application.

## What's an ORM?

An object relational mapper is a piece of software that can translate data between different formats for serialization. For instance, say you have a data model in JavaScript, with JavaScript's primitive data types: strings, numbers, and booleans. You want to persist your data in a MySQL database that wants to store that data in its supported types: CHAR, FLOAT, and BIT. An ORM knows how to translate your data to and from these differing formats so that you can serialize and de-serialize your data safely. ORMs have traditionally been a server-side technology, but Ember Data includes much ORM-like functionality on the client side. This allows you to separate the concerns of working with your data in your client-side application and persist your data to a long-term persistence solution (server, file storage, etc.). In fact, Ember Data allows you to write adapters that provide a consistent API, such that you could switch from using dummy data in the form of an in-memory JavaScript object in the early stages of the project, to using a MySQL service during development, to using a PostgreSQL service in production, without ever changing your model, view, or controller code.

# What Is Ruby on Rails?

Ruby on Rails is a development platform made of two parts: Ruby, a programming language developed by Yukihiro "Matz" Matsumoto; and Ruby on Rails, a framework and set of conventions for building web applications in Ruby and a toolchain for the automated creation and maintenance of applications that adhere to those conventions, developed by David Heinemeier Hansson (DHH). Like Ember, Ruby on Rails espouses the "convention over configuration" approach. Its version of Ember's "Because this pattern is so common, it is the default" is DHH's "Look at all the things I'm *not* doing!" as seen in this Ruby on Rails demo (*http://bit.ly/1odZUh9*). We'll learn more about Ruby on Rails and why you might like to use it as your backend in Chapter 8.

# What Is Node.js?

When Google set out to build its own web browser, way back in 2008 (or probably earlier, because that's the year it was released), the team built its JavaScript engine, called V8, in such a way that it was, besides being quite fast, a great tool for hacking. People figured out pretty quickly that you could use it to create all manner of applications outside a browser and written in JavaScript that could have many of the features of "native" applications, such as disk access or hardware inputs and outputs. Perhaps the most popular project to come out of this wizardry is Node.js, an application platform built on V8 that is particularly good at building scalable applications that run across multiple CPUs, due to its event-driven design. It's not just for building web servers, but it has become quite popular for that purpose. And if you *are* building a web server with Node.js, you'll probably want to take a look at...

## Express.js

Express.js (*http://expressjs.com*) is a web-application framework for Node.js applications that does a lot of the heavy lifting in creating web applications. Rather than writing an HTTP server from scratch, Express can provide you a lot of off-the-shelf functionality, while giving you plenty of opportunity to customize or overwrite the features you need.

# CHAPTER 2

# The Basics

In this chapter, we'll start out with the traditional "Hello, world!" then backtrack to see all the work Ember did for us under the covers. We'll also take a look at what tools and software you'll need to get started.

## Hello, World Wide Web

If you haven't already, head to *emberjs.com* in your browser. Click the big, orange—at the time of this writing—"Download the starter kit" link. While it's downloading, bookmark the Guides link in the navigation bar at the top of the page. It may not be the absolute best place to start, but the guide linked there is an excellent second or third lesson on Ember. The Getting Started video on the first page, though, is definitely worth your time and makes as good a starting point as it does a refresher.

Once that starter kit has downloaded, take a look at the contents. You should see:

*css (folder)*

> *normalize.css*
>> As the maker explains (*http://necolas.github.io/normalize.css/*), "Normalize.css makes browsers render all elements more consistently and in line with modern standards. It precisely targets only the styles that need normalizing."

> *style.css*
>> A place for you to put your style declarations.

*index.html*
> A nice HTML file set up for you with all the JavaScript and stylesheets correctly imported and a couple example templates in place.

*js (folder)*

> *libs (folder)*
>> Contains Ember, jQuery, and Handlebars.

> *app.js*
>> This is where your application will live.

Go ahead and open up the *index.html* file—on any modern platform I can think of, this is as easy as double-clicking/tapping the file, no web server required—and ensure that your browser is able to render the page. If you're having any trouble at this point, it's likely that you have an unusual setting selected in your browser, such as disabling JavaScript. You should see something like Figure 2-1.

*Figure 2-1. The Ember starter kit*

Now open the *index.html* file in your favorite development editor. Inside the body tag you'll find your first (and second, actually) Handlebars template. We'll come back to that in a bit. For now, let's just take note of a few things about the two templates on the page. First, notice that they're contained within `script` tags with the type `text/x-handlebars`. That type differs from the usual `text/javascript`, and it tells the browser not to try to interpret the contents as JavaScript; so while the contents of these `script` tags will live on the page and be accessible from JavaScript, they will not be executed or rendered by the browser, at least not until you do it yourself, or until Ember and Handlebars do it for you.

Notice that in each template you see mostly plain old HTML, such as the h2 tag in the first template and ul tag in the second. You'll also see examples of some Handlebars directives: outlet in the first template, and lots of fun things in the second. Handlebars will replace these with plain HTML before putting them into the body tag of your document.

Keep that HTML file open, and now also open the *app.js* file. The page we loaded a moment ago may not look like much, but consider what's happening:

1. An HTML page with *no* literal content in its body tag is loaded.
2. Then, a JavaScript framework comes along, instantiates an application, a router, a route, and a model explicitly, as well as a couple controllers and views implicitly.
3. Then, it loads a couple templates that were embedded within the HTML page.
4. And finally, it processes those templates, interpolating model data and rendering all of it to the page.

What's more, as we'll see later, the templates are "live." If you were to pop into the console in your browser and change the contents of the model to include "green," you'd see a new list item added immediately to the page. Likewise, if you removed "blue," it would immediately disappear. And you didn't even have to write an event handler.

But we're a little ahead of ourselves. Let's see how minimal Ember can get. Before we start monkeying with our starter kit, though, we'll want to talk a little bit about web servers. If you know your way around an Apache or Nginx *.conf* file, go ahead and fire up your server of choice and skip the next subsection. If you're new to web servers, don't worry: there's a simple option.

# SimpleHTTPServer: Just Like It Says on the Tin

"But why do we need a web server?" you might be thinking. "Can't I just keep double-clicking the *index.html* file like I have been so far?"

You absolutely could, but you'll quickly run into caching troubles. You'll find yourself editing your project and hitting refresh in your browser but not seeing any changes. This is because your browser is caching the requests for *index.html*, *style.css*, *app.js*, and the rest. You can keep making changes, but the browser is going to keep loading its old copy, until it decides, of mostly its own accord, to refresh its copy. A good web server will intermediate for you, letting the browser know it's got a newer version of the file than the browser has.

Python offers a handy web server for development purposes that will aggressively monitor your files for changes. If you're on a Mac (10.2 or later), you already have

Python installed. If you're on Windows, you can download a click-through installer (*http://www.python.org*) that will have you running in minutes.

Directions for the installation and configuration of Python could be its own, potentially short, assuredly profitless book. Again, if you're using a Mac, there's a very good chance it's already installed, as OS X has included it by default for several versions now. If you're running Windows, the YouTube video "How to Install Python on Windows 7" (*http://www.youtube.com/watch?v=L5t5U0XnSew*) may be of use.

If you get as far as installing Python on any computer but a Mac, you've already discovered your system's command line. If you're on a Mac and you've never used the Terminal application before, you can refer to the Treehouse article, "Introduction to the Mac OS X Command Line" (*http://bit.ly/1qRacrt*).

From a command line in a Python-enabled environment, calling `python -m Sim pleHTTPServer` from any directory will start up a web server with that directory as its root. If you have, for instance, a file there named *index.html*, you can then go to *http://localhost:8000* in your browser and see that HTML file rendered. If the "localhost" or ":8000" parts are new to you, check out the following sidebar.

`python -m SimpleHTTPServer` is no longer supported in Python 3. It has been merged into http.server, with the command `python -m http.server`.

## http://localwhosit:whatnow?

If you're new to the networking aspect of web development, it can be overwhelming. Getting myriad devices with different physical connections—from modems (yes, they are still in use in some places) to Ethernet to WiFi to LTE—running all manner of platforms and software—from Windows to Mac OS X to iOS to Java to machine code —to all talk to one another via one protocol is one of the greatest accomplishments of human history, if you ask us. Part of getting them to be able to talk to one another is giving each of them a unique address—something like a phone number—called an Internet Protocol (IP) address. A given device can have anywhere from zero to dozens of them. Typically you'll have a few.

Some IP addresses are dummy addresses that allow you to talk to yourself, in a manner of speaking. The address 127.0.0.1 is a special address reserved for just that: calling up your own computer. If you're running a web server with common configuration, putting that address into a browser will result in loading content right off your own device. Just as phone numbers can include an extension—some extra address information that indicates a specific phone line within a location that all shares the same main line, IP addresses can specify a port. You'll see them tacked onto the end of an IP address with a colon, like this: 127.0.0.1:80. If you don't specify a port, the default port 80 is implied, so 127.0.0.1 is actually the same as 127.0.0.1:80. It's a lot like calling a main phone number and getting the front desk; port 80 is the "main" page of your site.

Now, we obviously got away from just using IP addresses to navigate the Web; we use uniform resource locators (URLs). Special servers somewhere between your computer and the server you're trying to reach intercept your request for "google.com" and translate that into a request for an IP address (74.125.225.231, in the case of Google). Within your own operating system (more than likely) is a similar mechanism that will translate a request for "localhost" into a request for 127.0.0.1. Try it as soon as you're sure you have a server running. Type **http://localhost** into the address bar of your browser.

With both URLs and "localhost" you can still specify a port, too, such as "google.com:80" or "localhost:8000."

# Data Binding

Now that we know our changes will show up, go ahead and comment out all lines but the first line in *app.js* and reload the page. You should still see "Welcome to Ember.js" but no longer see the list of colors. Take a moment and look at what remains in both your HTML and JS files. There's not much there, and yet quite a bit is still happening in your browser. Don't forget that the h2 tag with "Welcome to Ember.js" isn't actually *in* your HTML content but is "hidden" from the renderer in a script tag that isn't actually being interpreted as a script tag.

So with one line of JavaScript remaining, you still have an application that's doing all that impressive stuff we outlined six paragraphs back. See for yourself; comment out that first line of JavaScript and see the empty page as a result. With just that one line in place, we're not explicitly defining a router or route anymore (we don't know what those are, yet, but they sound awfully important), but Ember is still creating them for us, for the mere price of instantiating an Ember Application object defined in a single line of code. For more on the Ember router and routes, stay tuned for additional details in Chapter 5.

OK, let's start tinkering to get an introduction to data binding. First, let's add a second line that creates an ill-advised (don't do this in production) global variable, like this:

```
App.model = ['red', 'yellow', 'blue'];
```

Now change what should be line 18 or so in your HTML from this:

```
{{#each item in model}}
```

to this:

```
{{#each item in App.model}}
```

Reload your browser, and you should see what you saw the first time you loaded it: the welcome message and the list of colors. Now fire up your console (if that's an unfamiliar concept, watch this video series (*http://bit.ly/1qRauyz*)) and execute this JavaScript:

```
App.set('model',['red','yellow','blue','green']);
```

As soon as you hit Enter, a new `li` tag was added to the page with the contents `green`. If you've ever had to write the kind of code that makes such real-time synchronization—or binding—possible, you're probably impressed, maybe even relieved.

Let's see it work in the other direction. In your *index.html* file, replace what should be line 12 or so with this:

```
<h2>Welcome to {{view Ember.TextField valueBinding="App.name"}}</h2>
```

There's some new stuff there, but for now let's just say that this tells Ember to render an `input` tag whose `value` attribute will be bound to `App.name`. This input field and the `App.name` variable will "watch" each other, notifying each other of changes in their values and updating their own copy when they observe a change. Speaking of, we need to create that `App.name` object. Add the following as the third line of *app.js*:

```
App.name = "Tom Waits";
```

Reload the page, and you'll see an input form field within our `h2` tag, pre-populated with "Tom Waits." If we pop open the console and change `App.name` like we did a moment ago with `App.set('name','A new value')`, you would see the value of this `in put` tag immediately change. This time, though, see what happens if you edit the contents of that `input` tag. Go ahead; click into the form field and change it to something like "Susan Tedeschi." Now, in your console, execute this code to see the current contents of the `App.name` property:

```
App.get('name');
```

The console's response should be "Susan Tedeschi" or whatever you entered into your `input` tag. You just edited a property of the model within your route (and, again, we don't even know what that is, yet, but we will soon enough), right from the comfort of a web form! This is two-way data binding, and it's one of the main reasons to use Ember. Throughout your application development, you can skip worrying about synchronizing changes between model properties and view entities. Ember's got it covered.

# But Where's All the Code?

We've already seen a lot of functionality, and we've barely written any code. What's more, we haven't even *seen* much code. A lot of frameworks offer generators that will automatically generate whole swaths of your project for you, based on conventions. Ruby on Rails is famous for this feature, generating models, views, controllers, and even database records for you with a single command at the terminal. The result of this command, though, is a project folder full of new files—your new models, views, controllers, and so on. Ember is different.

When you fire up an Ember `Application` object, Ember will immediately search your code for implementations of an `ApplicationRoute`, an `ApplicationController`, and either a template with the attribute `data-template-name="application"` or the first template on the page with no `data-template-name` specified. As we demonstrated earlier, if it doesn't find those first two things—your own class definitions for a route and a controller—it will create default instances. What we haven't mentioned is that this happens in memory. No files are generated.

The bad news is that this makes it a little more difficult to inspect these objects and learn the innards of Ember. This is certainly still possible, in more ways than one, but it's not as easy as opening up generated files the way you would in a Ruby on Rails application. The good news is that when a new version of Ember is released, you don't have to update dozens or hundreds of files on your web server, at least not to incorporate the changes to Ember itself. You can simply swap in the new *ember-x-x-x.js* file, and the next time you fire up your app, it will be running in a brand-new Ember environment. This doesn't mean you won't have any work to do, necessarily. If the Ember API changes, you'll definitely have to modify your classes to reflect those changes.

# Uh, What's a Router?

We just threw some terms at you from out of nowhere, didn't we? (In case you're curious, the hardest part of writing this book was figuring out whether to start with the chicken or the egg.) We talked a bit in Chapter 1 about models, views, and controllers. Many web-application frameworks add another pillar to that trio, called a router. In the old days, when we were young, we used web servers that simply responded to URL requests—someone visiting a particular URL that was within your domain—by associating them with folder structures. So, for instance, everything after the first forward slash in the URL could be easily translated to folders on your server's hard drive: *http://www.somethingclever.com/folder/inner-folder/index.html* would tell your web server to go to the root of your web documents folder and locate a folder named *folder*, an *inner-folder* folder within that and, finally, a file named *index.html*.

When you're building a web application, though, you're not typically dealing with folders full of static files. You could be dealing with a single HTML file—thus the "single-page apps" craze. We do, however, want to continue to use unique URLs to capture specific states or entry points to our applications. So, whatever it was that existed in our old web servers, like Apache, that could turn *http://blahblahblah.com/*

*stuff/index.html* into a reference to *C:\docroot\stuff\index.html* will need to be rebuilt in our fancy, new JavaScript applications. That thing, in fact, is called a router.

In your routers, and you *will* be writing plenty of them, you will declare nearly every URL to which you wish your application to respond. If you don't declare a URL, your application will not know how or even that it *should* respond to a request for that resource. We'll look at how exactly you do that later.

You might be wondering how everything can fit in a router. After all, if some form of the logic for how to respond to every single URL for your application is all stored in the router, it must be possible to very quickly have a router that is thousands of lines of code long. Doesn't sound like it would scale well, does it? No, it wouldn't. This is why the router mostly just associates URLs with routes. Routes store the logic necessary to get your application to—and from—the state represented by the URL. So, for now, whenever you see "router" and "routes," just think, "the stuff that translates URLs to application states and back."

Pretty important stuff. I'm kind of surprised that people don't call frameworks like Ember MVRC, for model-view-router-controller.

# Ember in Action

Let's restore our starter kit code to "factory settings"; delete lines 2 and 3 and uncomment the original code that came with the starter kit. Your *app.js* file should now look just like it did when you downloaded it:

```
App = Ember.Application.create();

App.Router.map(function() {
  // put your routes here
});

App.IndexRoute = Ember.Route.extend({
  model: function() {
    return ['red', 'yellow', 'blue'];
  }
});
```

Be sure to change your *index.html* file back to its original state to match. You can always download a new copy of the starter kit if you've lost track (or revert your changes—you *are* using source control, right?).

Let's step through what happens when you load *http://localhost:8000* in your browser:

1. The HTML page loads, which loads and executes your *app.js* file.

2. *app.js* instantiates an Ember `Application`.

3. When the `Application` starts up, it immediately looks to see if you've written your own `ApplicationRoute`, loading it if there is one, and loading its own either way (your class, if you wrote one, extends the default class).

4. The `Application` does the same load-yours-too-if-you-wrote-one routine with `ApplicationController`.

5. If you've defined your own `ApplicationRoute`—and defined any event hooks within that should be fired (such as an `activate` definition)—they will now be fired.

6. Ember then looks for an application template in your HTML and sets it up with `ApplicationController` as its controller, which we'll see later becomes the conduit through which data flows into your templates, replacing placeholders with live data.

7. Because we are at the root URL of your application (given that no route in particular is specified), Ember will now locate and instantiate the `IndexRoute` you specified in *app.js*.

8. Ember will now identify that you didn't specify an `IndexController` and will instantiate one for you. We'll go into more detail about this later, but Ember has some choices to make about what kind of default controller will be most useful. Because you defined a model in `IndexRoute` that is an array, Ember will instantiate an `ArrayController` as your `IndexController`.

9. Ember will find the template named *index* in the HTML document and render it to the `outlet` helper in our application template (we'll cover what helpers and that funny outlet thing are in the next chapter).

This may be something like the 73rd time we've said this, but keep in mind, *this all happened with 11 lines of code*, and almost the exact same thing happened when there was just one line of code. This highlights the mantra we mentioned in Chapter 1. Nearly the same thing happens with one line of code as with 11 because we only defined one thing—our model—that wasn't a default object/feature. In the words of the Ember.js guides, "Because this pattern is so common, it is the default for…" And because it is the default, you don't even have to write that code out.

One more example, and then we'll start in earnest on dissecting Ember. We're going to cover a lot of things very quickly that we haven't actually discussed, yet, so don't worry if you see terms you don't know. We'll get there. This is a brisk walk through the way Ember works, which we'll then do again very slowly.

Let's say you clicked into the address bar right now, changing the address to *http://localhost:8000/examples/1*. Pop quiz: what would Ember do?

You're right. It's a trick question. Ember would do nothing, because you've loaded a page that doesn't exist. You'd see an error message from the Python SimpleHTTP-Server (Figure 2-2).

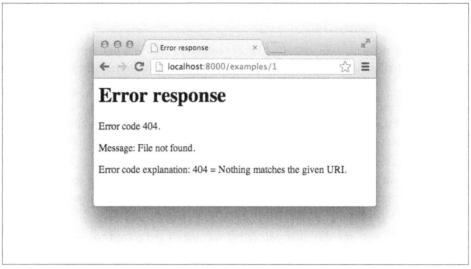

*Figure 2-2. Error message from the Python SimpleHTTPServer*

Important lesson, hopefully learned: by default, you have to use a hash in your route URLs. The URL we just tried is one that specifies a file in a folder which can be served by a traditional web server. We only have one file, so our URLs aren't actually pointing at separate files or folders. When you insert a hash into a URL, the web server stops trying to interpret the URL as a file/folder structure at the point of the hash. You can put anything you like after that hash, and the server will not try to locate a file by that name. The page will, though, get the whole URL, and Ember knows how to turn the rest of that URL—the stuff beyond the hash—into a route.

So a good URL would be *http://localhost:8000/#/examples/1*. Loading that URL at this point will net you a blank browser window, because we haven't defined the route, but let's go through what Ember will look for:

1. First, all of the stuff in the previous list like this, and then:

2. Because of the */examples*, Ember will look for a route named `ExamplesRoute`.

3. Ember will look for or create an `ExamplesController`.

4. Ember will call the `model` function of `ExamplesRoute`, passing it the last portion of your URL, looking a bit like this, were you to define an `ExamplesRoute`:

```
model: function(params) {
        return App.Example.find(params.example_id);
}
```

5. Ember can now retrieve your model data and populate a template named *examples* in your HTML, rendering it to the `outlet` helper in your application template.

Stop me if you've heard this one, but because this pattern is so common, it is the default for route handlers, meaning the `model` function we just wrote isn't necessary, unless you're doing something other than what's written previously.

For the record, you can't actually execute this little thought experiment without a good bit more code than we actually wrote out here. Don't worry; we'll get there. This exercise was about seeing the naming conventions a few times, getting a feel for how Ember locates/creates things for you, and walking through the life cycle.

# Wrapping Things Up

So, that was a whirlwind tour through an Ember bootstrap sequence. Don't worry if it didn't all make sense. It wasn't meant to, yet. Think of it as the first day of a trip to a foreign country. You're jet-lagged and circling the town center in a cheesy tour bus, noting places to which you'd like to return over the next week between narcoleptic retreats and bleary-eyed gazes at nothing in particular.

Go get some coffee, take a nap, or run around the block and come back for the next chapter.

# CHAPTER 3

# Ember Boilerplate and Workflow

Now that we have a firm grasp of the basics of Ember applications, it is time to begin setting up a professional workflow. This is an important step in the process but isn't absolutely necessary. That being said, if you are interested in saving valuable time, creating a maintainable codebase, and preparing for testing, then it is recommended to do some initial work in setting up your development environment. You will thank us later.

At the time of this writing, and with the Ember 1.0 release, there are a number of tools available to manage boilerplate and workflow of Ember applications. Until tooling and workflow are a part of core, this will remain a bit confusing when choosing best practices. In the end, developer workflow and the tools used to manage it are highly subjective, a matter of preference, and controversial. We will take a neutral stance here by presenting only the facts.

Currently, there are four projects that provide varying degrees of functionality into workflow management and boilerplate-code creation:

*Yeoman's Ember Generator (https://github.com/yeoman/generator-ember)*
> Yeoman, a collection of tools, provides an Ember application generator and individual subgenerators for models, views, and controllers.

*Ember Tools (https://github.com/rpflorence/ember-tool)*
> A project created and maintained by Ryan Florence. The Ember community has stated that Ember Tools will be merged with Ember App Kit into core in the future. Ember Tools uses Browserify (*http://www.browserify.org*), a project by James Halliday that provides the capability to compile Node.js-style modules for use in the browser, to manage the JavaScript dependencies. You can also generate individual models, views, and controllers with Ember Tools.

*Ember App Kit (https://github.com/stefanpenner/ember-app-kit)*
> In the notes provided in the Ember 1.0 release, the Ember team stated: "EAK will eventually become the core of official Ember Tools."
>
> Currently an alternative to Yeoman, Ember App Kit is another toolset that you can use as a starting point for your project. At the time of this writing, EAK does take some manual setup. By cloning the project from GitHub and wiping out the existing Git history, Ember App Kit provides a vanilla boilerplate application that includes an integrated Grunt task runner along with Grunt tasks, such as JSHint, QUnit, and the Testem test runner. EAK also provides support for ECMAScript 6 modules through the inclusion of the ES6 Module Transpiler. ECMAScript 6 modules are coming in the next JavaScript version, but EAK allows you to get a head start by providing the necessary namespacing to keep your Ember classes out of global scope.
>
> EAK also ships with boilerplace for setting up stub APIs so that you can use Ember Data's RESTAdapter instead of the FixtureAdapter. This will make more sense in Chapter 7, when these topics are covered.
>
> Again, in Chapter 8, you will see more of EAK when we go into more detail on the specifics of developing a backend for your application.
>
> And finally, in Chapter 10, we will explore the specifics of the *out-of-the box* EAK testing setup. To follow along, checkout this EAK specific repo (*https://github.com/emberjsbook/rocknrollcall-eak*).

*Ember Rails (https://github.com/emberjs/ember-rails)*
> Ember Rails is a Ruby gem that provides support for Active Model Serializers, production copies of Ember, Ember Data, and handlebars, and integration with the Rails Asset Pipeline. More on Ember Rails is availble in Chapter 9.

*Ember CLI (http://iamstef.net/ember-cli/)*
> Ember CLI promises to replace Ember Tools and Ember App Kit in the future, as the official toolset for building Ember applications. At the time of this writing, it is not recommended to use for serious applications. The documentation states: "Although potentially exciting, this is still a work in progress project, so use at your own risk."
>
> Overall, Ember CLI is focused on improving developer productivity in a number of ways, such as modules, built-in testing, and dependency management.
>
> Perhaps one of the most exciting features of Ember CLI is that it uses Broccoli as an asset pipeline instead of Grunt's `watch` task. The advantage is that it rebuilds individual files instead of the entire Grunt project, therefore significantly decreasing build times.

Like Ember App Kit, it also uses the ES6 Module Transpiler, which turns ES6 module syntax into AMD modules.

To keep the scope of this text limited, we decided that at the time of writing the most complete solution for rapid prototyping was Yeoman. That being said, for Chapters 4–6, we will leverage Yeoman to build a prototype of our application.

In Chapters 7–10, we will introduce Ember App Kit and ember-rails gem for more specific, production-related use cases and topics.

# Git

First, let's cover version control.

We will be using Git for version control of the source code included within this book. We will also be using Github, the popular web-based hosting service for open source software development projects. Here, we will manage the source code of our demo application, RocknRollCall.

Also, as you will see later in this chapter, we will be setting up our application using the best combination of these tools. To get started, check out the GitHub repo for the RockNRollCall application (*http://bit.ly/1qRaRcr*) (see Figure 3-1).

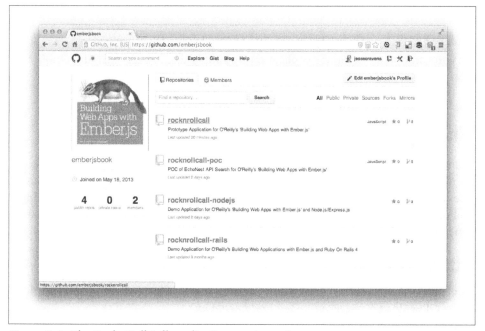

*Figure 3-1. The RocknRollCall application source code*

View the commit log on the master branch (*http://bit.ly/1odZirX*) to follow along as we build our application throughout the remainder of the book.

GitHub also provides social-networking functionality, such as feeds, followers, and the social-network graph to display how developers work on their versions of a repository. If you would like to follow updates, create an account (if you don't already have one), and click the Watch button at the top right of the repository page.

A complete overview of Git is out of the scope of this text, but if you are new to Git, here are a few resources to help you get started:

- *Version Control with Git* by Jon Loeliger and Matthew McCullough (O'Reilly, 2009)
- *Git Pocket Guide* by Richard E. Silverman (O'Reilly, 2013)

If you are creating the application from scratch, as you follow along, begin by making a directory:

```
$ mkdir rocknrollcall-yeoman
```

Then:

```
$ cd rocknrollcall-yeoman
```

After that, initialize a new local Git repository:

```
$ git init
```

Or you can obtain the entire application by simply cloning it from our remote GitHub repository:

```
$ git clone https://github.com/emberjsbook/rocknrollcall-yeoman.git
```

# What Is Yeoman?

Yeoman (*http://yeoman.io/*) is a bundle of web development tools that helps developers manage an efficient workflow, reduce manual boilerplate, and manage complexity. The Yeoman toolset consists of three tools: an application generator or scaffolding tool named Yo, Grunt.js as an integrated build tool, and Bower to manage application dependencies like the JavaScript and CSS libraries included in your project.

## Installing Yeoman

To get started, we need to install Node.js. To install Node.js, follow the guides on the project download page (*http://nodejs.org/download/*).

Included with Node.js is NPM (Node Package Manager). With NPM, we can install the three tools just described by using the following command:

```
$ npm install -g yo grunt-cli bower
```

There you have it. Now let's check our install by simply typing the following:

```
$ yo
```

After a brief offer to provide anonymous feedback, you will be prompted to make a decision. For now, you can choose "Get me out of here!" No worries, we will come back to this later:

```
[?] =========================================================================
We're constantly looking for ways to make yo better!
May we anonymously report usage statistics to improve the tool over time?
More info: https://github.com/yeoman/insight & http://yeoman.io
==========================================================================: No
[?] What would you like to do? (Use arrow keys)
  Install a generator
  Find some help
> Get me out of here!
```

# Using Yo's Ember Application Generator

Yo reduces the amount of time it takes to get started by generating boilerplate code for you. Yo also generates your Grunt configuration and relevant Grunt tasks that are recommended by the community. Also, as you will see, when we use the Ember generator, all of the tasks considered to be important are included in the interactive command prompts.

Now, let's get to our first order of business, generating an application.

## Installing Dependencies

We have a few dependencies we must install as well before we get started.

### Ruby

Before you use the generators, we will need to ensure that Ruby is installed (version 1.9.3 or higher). If you are on a Mac OS X, you should have Ruby by default. If you are on anything else, you will need to install Ruby.

You can check for the location and version of Ruby like this:

```
$ which ruby
/usr/bin/ruby

$ ruby -v
ruby 2.0.0p247 (2013-06-27 revision 41674) [universal.x86_64-darwin13]
```

### Compass

Compass is an open source authoring framework for the Sass CSS preprocessor. You will need Compass to run the Ember generators and compile Sass to CSS. To install:

```
$ gem install compass
```

Because we already installed Node.js and NPM, we can issue the following command to install a Grunt plug-in that contains a Compass Grunt task. The Ember generator will call this behind the scenes.

## Install the Generator

Now that we have Yeoman and all of our generator dependencies installed, we can begin to install the actual Ember generator. To get a sense of context, let's first take a look at all the generators available to us. Open a terminal and type the following:

```
$ npm search yeoman-generator
```

Be patient; this may take some time. Eventually, you should see something like the following results:

```
$ npm search yeoman-generator
npm WARN Building the local index for the first time, please be patient
npm http GET https://registry.npmjs.org/-/all

NAME                      DESCRIPTION                        AUTHOR
DATE            VERSION      KEYWORDS
calaxa                    calaxa ======                      =apathetic
2013-05-14 09:11  0.0.1       yeoman-generator sass compa
ft-wp                          Front-Trends Wordpress generator  =hubertburdach
2013-03-30 21:08  0.0.1       yeoman-generator web
generator-admo            A generator for Yeoman             =drubin
2014-02-04 09:07  0.9.5       yeoman-generator admo Digit
generator-android     Yeoman generator for Android        =groupsky
2014-01-17 09:03  0.1.0       yeoman-generator android sc
generator-angular-js  Yeoman generator for AngularJS     =doboy
2013-11-24 10:02  1.0.1       yeoman-generator scaffold f

... and so on.
```

At the time of writing, there are literally hundreds of generators written by the community for Yeoman, including everything from Android to Angular. But today, we are interested in Ember.js.

Now open up a new terminal and summon Yo:

```
$ yo
```

You should then see the following prompt:

```
[?] What would you like to do? (Use arrow keys)
❯ Update your generators
  Install a generator
  Find some help
  Get me out of here!
```

Obviously, we should choose "Install a generator." Next, we are presented with a prompt to search against NPM. So we will enter "ember" as our keyword. At the time of writing, you can see the Ember-related generators available in the repository:

```
[?] Search NPM for generators: ember
[?] Here's what I found. Install one? (Use arrow keys)
> generator-ember
  generator-ember-jade-zurb
  generator-ember-jade-zurb-express
  generator-ember-laravel
  generator-ember-less
  generator-ember-rk
  generator-jhipster-ember
  Search again
  Return home
```

Hit Enter and Yo will download and install all of the dependencies and inform us that the installation is complete:

```
I just installed your generator by running:
    npm install -g generator-ember
```

## Running the Generator

Now we are ready to run the generator, and we are presented with another prompt:

```
[?] What would you like to do? (Use arrow keys)
> Run the Ember generator (0.8.3)
  Run the Mocha generator (0.1.3)
  Update your generators
  Install a generator
  Find some help
  Get me out of here!
```

Choose "Run the Ember generator (0.8.3)" (note that the version may update by the time you read this). Again, Yo presents us with a number of questions:

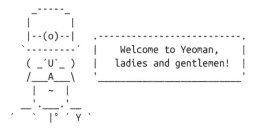

```
Would you like to include Twitter Bootstrap for Sass? (Y/n)
```

As we dont wan't to spend time on styling our application within the scope of this book, we will select Yes. Now, we will see a number of logs that indicate that our files are being created:

```
create .gitignore
create .gitattributes
create .bowerrc
create bower.json
create package.json
create .jshintrc
create .editorconfig
create Gruntfile.js
create app/templates/application.hbs
create app/templates/index.hbs
create app/index.html
create app/styles/style.scss
create app/scripts/app.js
invoke    mocha:app
create    test/index.html
create    test/lib/chai.js
create    test/lib/expect.js
create    test/lib/mocha/mocha.css
create    test/lib/mocha/mocha.js
create    test/spec/test.js
```

```
I'm all done. Running bower install & npm install for you to install the re
quired dependencies.
If this fails, try running the command yourself.
```

Now you should see a long list of logs. Here is a abbreviated example:

```
npm WARN package.json static-projects@0.0.0 No README.md file found!
npm http GET https://registry.npmjs.org/grunt
npm http GET https://registry.npmjs.org/grunt-contrib-copy
npm http GET https://registry.npmjs.org/grunt-contrib-concat
```

```
...
```

Let's now explore the filesystem to better understand what was created for us
(Figure 3-2). Notice the three top-level directories: *app*, *node_modules*, and *test*. The
*app* directory contains all of your application files, *node_modules* contains your application dependencies, and *test* contains your test files and the configuration files, such
as *.bowerrc*, *.gitignore*, *.jshintrc*, *Gruntfile.js*, and *package.json*. These files manage the
different levels of configuration within your application and development
environment.

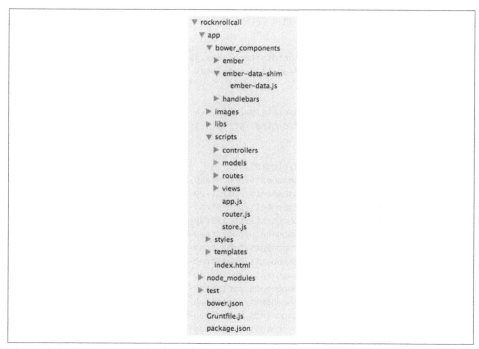

*Figure 3-2. The generated Ember filesystem*

## HTML

Also take a look at the *index.html* file within the *app* directory—a significant amount of boilerplate code has been generated: the HTML5 doctype, the Ember.js dependencies (in the correct load order), and the `build` comments used by Gruntfile.js to replace (or remove) references to nonoptimized scripts or stylesheets within HTML files:

```
<!doctype html>
<html>
    <head>
        <meta charset="utf-8">
        <title>Yeoman Ember Starter Kit</title>

        <!-- build:css styles/main.css -->
        <link rel="stylesheet" href="styles/style.css">
        <!-- endbuild -->
</head>
    <body>
        <!-- build:js(app) scripts/components.js -->
        <script src="bower_components/jquery/jquery.js"></script>
        <script src="bower_components/handlebars/handlebars.runtime.js">
        </script>
        <script src="@@ember"></script>
```

```
<script src="@@ember_data"></script>
<!-- endbuild -->

<!-- build:js(.tmp) scripts/templates.js -->
<script src="scripts/compiled-templates.js"></script>
<!-- endbuild -->

<!-- build:js(.tmp) scripts/main.js -->
<script src="scripts/combined-scripts.js"></script>
<!-- endbuild -->

<!-- build:js scripts/plugins.js -->
<script src="bower_components/bootstrap-sass/js/affix.js"></script>
<script src="bower_components/bootstrap-sass/js/alert.js"></script>
<script src="bower_components/bootstrap-sass/js/dropdown.js"></script>
<script src="bower_components/bootstrap-sass/js/tooltip.js"></script>
<script src="bower_components/bootstrap-sass/js/modal.js"></script>
<script src="bower_components/bootstrap-sass/js/transition.js"></script>
<script src="bower_components/bootstrap-sass/js/button.js"></script>
<script src="bower_components/bootstrap-sass/js/popover.js"></script>
<script src="bower_components/bootstrap-sass/js/carousel.js"></script>
<script src="bower_components/bootstrap-sass/js/scrollspy.js"></script>
<script src="bower_components/bootstrap-sass/js/collapse.js"></script>
<script src="bower_components/bootstrap-sass/js/tab.js"></script>
<!-- endbuild -->
</body>
</html>
```

A couple of really important things to notice are the *scripts/compiled-templates.js* and *scripts/combined-scripts.js* files wrapped in the build directives mentioned previously. Stay tuned; these files will be generated during our Grunt build later in our workflow.

## Basic Ember application

A basic Ember.js application was generated for us, in *app/scripts/app.js*. The application uses a `require` syntax to include other application dependencies (for more on `require` and JavaScript modularity, read Why Web Modules? (*http://requirejs.org/docs/why.html*)):

```
var Rocknrollcall = window.Rocknrollcall = Ember.Application.create();

/* Order and include as you please. */
require('scripts/controllers/*');
require('scripts/store');
require('scripts/models/*');
require('scripts/routes/*');
require('scripts/views/*');
require('scripts/router');
```

This modularity is a primary advantage of using a tool like Yeoman. If you were wondering why we didn't just download the starter kit, the answer is: we could have. We would have received very similar starter code all in one file, as we explored in Chapter 2:

```
RocknrollcallYeoman.ApplicationRoute = Ember.Route.extend({

  // admittedly, this should be in IndexRoute and not in the
  // top level ApplicationRoute; we're in transition... :-)

  model: function () {
    return ['red', 'yellow', 'blue'];
  }
});
```

If you explore the required scripts (controllers, store, models, routes, views, and router), you will see that all of the same functionality has been modularized out into separate files. This is a well-known, software design best practice known as the *separation of concerns*. This is a great example as to why we are using Yeoman to help us manage our code. Keep reading—there are more examples later.

## Using Bower

Much like Linux package managers, Bower manages your JavaScript libraries as packages, exposing versions to a CLI (command-line interface). Bower helps do dependency resolution so you get the exact right interoperable versions of all your libraries. This means that if one of your dependencies is redundant with a dependency of another, multiple versions of the script will not be included. For example, Ember.js is dependent on jQuery, but if you include another library that is dependent on jQuery, only one version will be loaded.

A *bower.json* file, similar to a Ruby Gemfile or Node.js *package.json*, is used to declare the dependencies used within a particular project:

```
{
  "name": "rocknrollcall-yeoman",
  "version": "0.0.0",
  "dependencies": {
    "ember": "1.3.2",
    "handlebars": "1.2.1",
    "ember-data": "1.0.0-beta.5",
    "ember-localstorage-adapter": "latest",
    "bootstrap-sass": "~3.0.0",
    "d3": "latest"
  },
  "devDependencies": {
    "ember-mocha-adapter": "0.1.2"
  }
}
```

At this point, you may be tempted to run your favorite local development server to deliver this application to your browser, like we did in Chapter 2. Just wait, however: among other things, Yeoman is going to help you with that as well.

# Grunt

So all of that was great so far, but now for the real time saver, Grunt.js. Grunt is a task runner that allows you to automate all of the tasks that you normally have to worry about on your own or with separate toolsets.

In the beginning of this book, we talked about efficiently building applications for production. Grunt is one of the core toolsets that enable this for us, by providing tasks that can do the following:

- Watch processes such as LiveReload
- Auto-compile CoffeeScript, Compass, and Sass
- Auto-lint
- Benchmark image optimization
- Generate an app cache manifest
- Minify and concatenate static resources
- Run a built-in preview server.

Gruntfile.js is the main configuration of your specific task setup. An entire book could be dedicated to Grunt.

For now, we will describe the general pattern of the setup. Gruntfile.js is fairly lengthy, so by breaking it down into digestable pieces, these are the core basics. The following methods are invoked from within the file:

`grunt.initConfig`

> The `initConfig` method provides the configuration for each of the tasks we register later in `grunt.registerTask()`.

For example, here is the basic config for one of our favorite tasks, `jshint`:

```
grunt.initConfig({
    yeoman: yeomanConfig,
    jshint: {
        options: {
            jshintrc: '.jshintrc',
            reporter: require('jshint-stylish')
        },
        all: [
            'Gruntfile.js',
            '<%= yeoman.app %>/scripts/{,*/}*.js',
```

```
                    '!<%= yeoman.app %>/scripts/vendor/*',
                    'test/spec/{,*/}*.js'
                ]
            },
        });
```

`grunt.loadNpmTasks`

> Before we register our tasks, we then need to load them as Node.js modules. This `require` declaration runs the `load-grunt-tasks` task that loads all the other tasks in the directory:

```
        require('load-grunt-tasks')(grunt);
```

Now that the dependencies are available, the Yeoman-generated Gruntfile includes the `register` calls for each task:

```
        grunt.registerTask('default', [
            'jshint'
        ]);
```

# Build, Run, Test

Finally, here are the Grunt-provided commands you can use to build, run, and test your application via the command line.

First, make sure you are in the directory of your application to run the following commands.

If you want to just build the application, you can run:

```
    $ grunt
```

Next, if we want to also view the app, we can run the preview server while watching changes to directories:

```
    $ grunt serve
```

This should fire up the application and run it in your web browser on *http://localhost: 9000* (Figure 3-3).

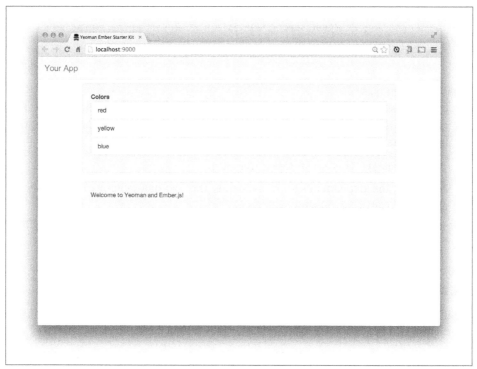

*Figure 3-3. Ember Starter Application with the Yeoman Ember Generator*

Finally, you should see the following output from Grunt in the console:

```
$ grunt serve
Running "serve" task

Running "clean:server" (clean) task
Cleaning .tmp...OK

Running "replace:app" (replace) task
Replace app/index.html -> .tmp/index.html

Running "concurrent:server" (concurrent) task

    Running "emberTemplates:dist" (emberTemplates) task
    File ".tmp/scripts/compiled-templates.js" created.

    Done, without errors.

    Running "compass:server" (compass) task
    directory .tmp/styles/
       create .tmp/styles/style.css (1.932s)
    Compilation took 1.935s
```

```
    Done, without errors.

Running "neuter:app" (neuter) task

Running "copy:fonts" (copy) task
Copied 4 files

Running "connect:livereload" (connect) task
Started connect web server on localhost:9000.

Running "open:server" (open) task

Running "watch" task
Waiting...
```

Later, in Chapter 10, you will see that we can also run tests from Grunt.

For now, you can get a small taste of testing, from the one Mocha test included in *app/test/spec/test.js*:

```
(function () {
    'use strict';

    describe('Give it some context', function () {
        describe('maybe a bit more context here', function () {
            it('should run here few assertions', function () {

            });
        });
    });
})();
```

Run the following:

```
$ grunt test
```

You should see this output from our Mocha tests:

```
Running "mocha:all" (mocha) task
Testing: http://localhost:9000/index.html

  1 passing (104ms)

>> 1 passed! (0.10s)
```

If you were building your own application as you followed along, then this will complete our basic Yeoman-generated and managed application.

Then add all of your changes to update the index using the current content found in the working tree. This stages the changes for the next commit:

```
$ git add .
```

Now commit these changes with a friendly message:

```
$ git commit -m "Initial commit"
```

That's it. Now, that we have a generated-application structure and an initial codebase complete with package management and a task runner, let's explore some more tooling: subgenerators.

# Debugging with the Ember Inspector for Chrome and Firefox

The Ember Inspector is a plug-in that aids developers in the debugging of Ember applications. Currently, the tools are limited to Chrome and Firefox. To obtain the plugin for Chrome developer tools, go to the download page (*http://bit.ly/1keL9cz*) (Figure 3-4).

*Figure 3-4. Ember Inspector extension for Google Chrome*

And for Firefox, go to this download page (*http://mzl.la/1ooUcvS*) (Figure 3-5).

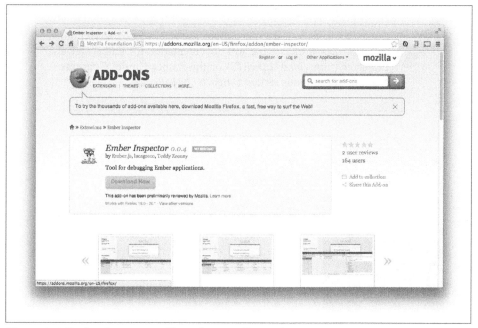

*Figure 3-5. Ember Inspector add-on for Mozilla Firefox*

Follow the individual browser's installation instructions, and we should be ready to begin debugging our Ember application. First, let's start with all of the routes defined in our application.

Because we haven't yet built our application, we can clone the finished application to demonstrate.

Make a new directory and migrate into it:

```
$ mkidr demo-inspector && cd demo-inspector
```

Then clone the finished repo:

```
$ git clone https://github.com/emberjsbook/rocknrollcall-yeoman.git
```

Now, use Grunt to serve up the application:

```
$ grunt serve
```

You now have the full functioning application within the *demo-inspector* directory. Once you are finished with our walkthrough of the inspector's features, you can move back to the original directory by:

```
$ cd ..
```

One of the most powerful aspects of the Ember Inspector is that it provides a built-in reference to all of Ember's naming conventions, as you can see in Figure 3-6.

### Ember's Naming Conventions

If you just want to learn more about Ember's naming conventions and how they work, see the API documentation for Ember.DefaultResolver (*http://bit.ly/1qRcBT3*) or the Ember Guides Concepts - Naming Conventions section (*http://bit.ly/1qRcEy2*).

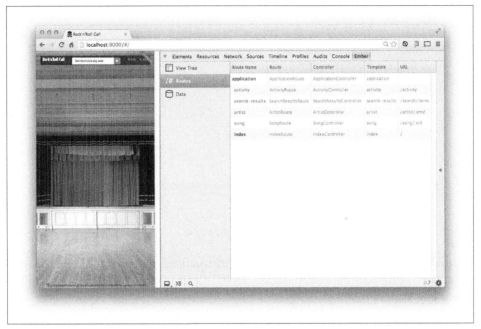

*Figure 3-6. Ember Inspector: naming conventions*

Also, once you have a number of routes and controllers within your application, you can view them and all of their respective properties individually. Figure 3-7 shows an example of inspecting a route's properties.

Then, inspect the View Tree tab and an overlay appears with the templates, controllers, and models associated to the current "state" of the rendered application, as shown in Figure 3-8. This is especially helpful when trying to determine if you have access to the correct model within a template.

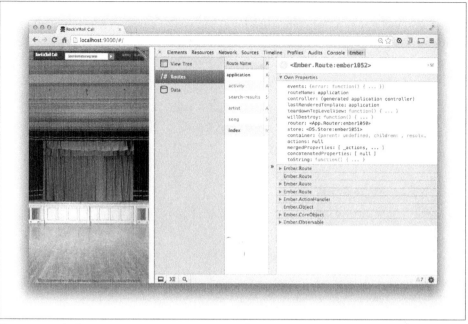

*Figure 3-7. Ember Inspector: inspecting a route's properties*

*Figure 3-8. Ember Inspector: inspecting the View Tree*

The Ember Inspector also helps greatly with your data layer. If Ember Data is installed, you will notice a Data tab. Click here, and view a current snapshot of all of the records currently stored in Ember Data, shown in Figure 3-9.

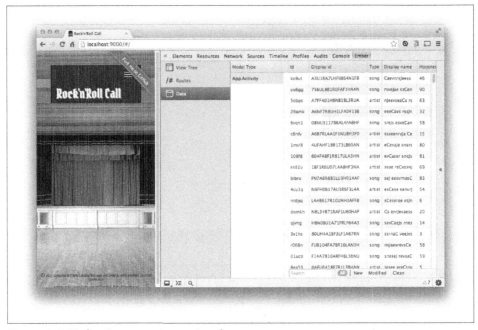

*Figure 3-9. Ember Inspector: inspecting data*

And finally, you can log out your application's objects to the console as the $E variable, shown in Figure 3-10.

*Figure 3-10. Ember Inspector: inspecting the application object*

# Wrapping Things Up

In Chapter 4, we will begin the *early design* phase: we'll begin to architect our solution by thinking through and diagramming the various *states* of the application and creating fake data. In parallel, we can also start building the first evolution of our application's Handlebars templates. If we are working with a team, we can also hand this task off to anyone that can write HTML/CSS while we begin to build the application logic.

# CHAPTER 4

# Building the RocknRollCall Prototype: Templates

In Chapter 3, we learned about modern workflow tools that take the guesswork and gruntwork out of setting up complex web applications. Now that we have a nicely organized project set up, it's time to start writing some code.

In this chapter, we'll focus on the templating system—Handlebars.js—that comes along with a default Ember setup. It's always tough to figure out where to start explaining a system like this, with so many interdependent "chickens" and "eggs," but we chose to start with the templating angle because that's where we think you should actually start an ambitious project. By the time you turn the last page in this chapter, you'll know how to inject "live" (two-way-bound) variables into an HTML template, how to automatically generate (and re-generate/update) HTML lists (UL and OL tags) from array references, and even how to use some logic (if/then/else) in your templates.

## Rock 'n' Roll

When it comes time to write an application for the purposes of demonstrating a new framework or an idea for how to write applications, it seems that writing a to-do application is the only choice. We wonder if that has something to do with the culture of Silicon Valley. We live in Austin, TX, sometimes called "Silicon Hills" because so many technology companies have moved some or all of their offices from California to Austin. They come here for many reasons, including far more affordable land and labor, but we can't help but think the pace is part of the draw. And so, to demonstrate, our demo application will not be a productivity application. We will build something akin to The Internet Movie Database (*http://imdb.com*) that indexes bands and musicians rather than films, directors, and actors. We call it "Rock'n'Roll Call." Besides, there's already a great Ember to-do demo application at TodoMVC (*http://todomvc.com/architecture-examples/emberjs*).

For such an app to be useful, it has to provide at least these features:

*The user should be able to search for artists and songs by name*
> Ideally, users should not have to specify that they are searching for an artist or a song; they should just be able to type in their search terms and hit "go."

*Search results should be displayed with an indication of what type of entity was found (i.e., artist or song)*
> We do not want to encumber users by requiring them to specify whether they wanted to search for an artist or song, but the results should probably have filters so that users can at that point, if they so desire, narrow their results to just artists or just songs.

*Search results should link to a page with more details about the found entity*
> It would be great if this page included a short description of the search result—a biography of an artist or a history of the song, as well as links to further information and even online media.

*For fun, let's also enable users to track the popularity of the music and musicians they search for, so users can gauge how "pop" their tastes may be*
> We'll need to persist such data somewhere, and ideally we would have some novel way of visualizing this data.

Obviously, we're going to need a *lot* of music data in order to pull this off. Perhaps the best thing about using this application, rather than a to-do list application, as our example, is that this app would be nearly impossible to build all on its own. To-do apps are islands—there needn't be any data that isn't generated by the user. This application, like most you will end up building in real-world development, will rely on interfacing with web services—other people's servers providing data. In this case, we built this application to talk to The Echo Nest (*http://the.echonest.com*), an excellent "music intelligence" service with a robust feature set, an enormous and growing database, great documentation, and a JavaScript API.

Spoiler alert—here's how we're going to pull all of this off:

1. We'll create a template that has an Ember TextField, bound to a variable we'll call searchTerms, with an `action` defined in the ApplicationController that will transition to a `SearchResultsRoute`, whose `SearchResultsController` will query the Echo Nest API with the searchTerms variable.

   `SearchResultsController` will query the Echo Nest API twice, once assuming the user is searching by artist name and once searching by song title.

2. Our `search-results` template will iterate over the search results separately, applying classnames that let us visualize the artists and songs in discrete ways.

Our `search-results` template will include a couple Ember Checkbox input helpers, and the display of our list of artist search results and song search results will be conditionally rendered based on the values of those checkboxes.

3. Echo Nest search results include unique IDs for the entities that match the search results. Our `search-results` template will include `link-to` helpers that will link to routes specifically set up to show a detailed view of artists (`ArtistRoute`) and songs (`SongRoute`). These routes will make an additional query on the Echo Nest API, requesting entity information and passing the unique ID associated with the link the user clicked from the search results list.

   Armed with a model generated from the Echo Nest response, the `ArtistView` or `SongView` will render, pulling images, video, and textual depictions of the entity from the Echo Nest response and populating the `artist` or `song` template.

4. When the user clicks on a search result, the `SearchResultsController` will write a record to local storage, capturing a timestamp, and the unique ID, display name, type, and "hotttnesss"—Echo Nest's proprietary measure of how popular an entity may be—of the entity. Later we'll look at persisting that data remotely.

   A link in the main navigation will lead the user to an `ActivityRoute` and `activity` template, which will include a component that makes use of D3 to visualize the user's activity—all the data captured as they've used the application. Because we're visualizing something called "hotttnesss," we think a heat map is an appropriate visualization scheme.

# Starting with HTML

If you've paid any attention to the topic of modern web development workflows, you've heard conversation lately about the increasing irrelevance of traditional workflows and approaches. "Waterfall" is becoming more and more a dirty word. The very tools used and artifacts created during development have been called into question. Mocking up a design for a responsive web application with Photoshop, for instance, creating renderings of your site at the myriad widths and heights that a browser may choose (or be constrained) to render your site within, is a never-ending task. Designing for ideal devices—large desktop monitors and powerful processors—simply doesn't cut it anymore.

When possible, your best bet is to design within the browser. If you are a designer who can write just enough HTML and CSS to mock up your designs, that is great. If you're a developer working with a designer who is not so confident with HTML and CSS, it's in your best interest to make yourself available to build these mockups early and often. And this is one of the great things about Ember's typical implementation: your templates are written in HTML.

For this application, rather than starting with wireframes or visual mockups, we actually mocked up our ideas in HTML and CSS. Having been at this for many years, this was a bit of a new experience for us. Most of the time our work feels like that of a building contractor being handed blueprints and going in with a nailgun and a pile of lumber, but this process felt more like being a sculptor—like the HTML was so much clay that we could push and pull around until it started to look the way we wanted it to.

# The Basics of Handlebars.js

You can start your project by simply building plain old static HTML. You'll come back and swap in Handlebars helpers and fold in conditionals and bound variables later. Let's start by building the global content in our application: the header, global parts of the page body, and the footer. We can simply add code like this—which makes use of Twitter Bootstrap—right into our *app/templates/application.hbs*:

```
<div class="wrapper">
  <div class="navbar navbar-inverse" role="navigation">
    <div class="navbar-header">
      <button type="button" class="navbar-toggle" data-toggle="collapse"
          data-target="#navbar-collapse-1">
        <span class="sr-only">Toggle navigation</span>
        <span class="icon-bar"></span>
        <span class="icon-bar"></span>
        <span class="icon-bar"></span>
      </button>
      <a href="#" class="navbar-brand">Rock'n'Roll Call</a>
    </div>

    <div id="navbar-collapse-1" class="collapse navbar-collapse">
      <ul class="nav navbar-nav search-lockup">
        <li class="search-group">
          <input class="search-input" placeholder="Search for artists or song
          names">
          <button class="btn btn-primary"><i class="glyphicon
          glyphicon-play"></i></button>
        </li>
      </ul>
      <ul class="nav navbar-nav navbar-right">
        <li><a href="#">Activity</a></li>
      </ul>

    </div>
  </div>

  <div class="container-fluid">
    <div class="row-fluid">
      <!-- page content here -->
    </div>
  </div>
```

```
      </div>
    </div>
    <footer>
      <p>
        <i class="glyphicon glyphicon-copyright-mark"></i> 2013 Companion to
        O'Reilly's
            <em>Building Web Apps with Ember.js: Write Ambitious Javascript</em>
            <a href="http://twitter.com/emberbook">@emberbook</a>
      </p>
      <p>
        Authors: Jesse Cravens <a href="http://twitter.com/jdcravens">@jdcravens</a>
            and Thomas Q. Brady <a href="http://twitter.com/thomasqbrady">@thomasq-
brady</a>
      </p>
    </footer>
```

And because this book isn't really about CSS, we will go ahead and add all of the site's CSS at once.

See the change in this commit (*http://bit.ly/1rEJ5Ql*).

### Twitter Bootstrap

If you are wondering how Twitter Bootstrap was included in your application, it was injected by Yeoman in Chapter 3, after we selected Y at this prompt:

```
Would you like to include Twitter Bootstrap for Sass?
(Y/n)
```

Figure 4-1 shows what the site looks like at the moment.

*Figure 4-1. Our barebones site, with a generous helping of CSS*

## Should I Use <script> Tags or .hbs Files?

In Chapter 2, we embedded Handlebars templates within the HTML pages, inside
<script> tags that looked like this one:

```
<script type="text/x-handlebars" data-template-name="application">
  <!-- template code here -->
</script>
```

This was possible because we were using the complete Handlebars build, which includes logic that, at runtime, searches for these <script> tags and converts them to
JavaScript objects—factories, really—in memory (in *Em.TEMPLATES*, if you're curious), ready to crank out markup based on your specification.

As you can imagine, that conversion from <script> tag to factory can get expensive,
especially as your application, and the number of templates within, grows. That's why
Handlebars allows for pre-compiling your templates and including only a honed *han-
dlebars.runtime.js* file, which leaves out the conversion logic, saving the time needed
to search out templates, and the download footprint of your application.

Because of the work we did to set up Yeoman in Chapter 2, we can use the racecar version of Handlebars. Yo will generate Handlebars templates for us, in its own discrete files with a *.hbs* extension, in conjunction with generating views; and Grunt will watch those templates for us, compiling them into JavaScript classes and concatenating them with the rest of our JavaScript each time we save changes.

You will just need to tell Grunt that you want it to watch your Ember templates, and you'll need to tell Grunt where to find them, like so:

```
grunt.initConfig({
    yeoman: yeomanConfig,
    watch: {
        emberTemplates: {
            files: '<%= yeoman.app %>/templates/**/*.hbs',
            tasks: ['emberTemplates', 'connect:livereload']
        }
    }
})
```

So to answer your question, move to *.hbs* files as soon as you can for production work, but <script> tags are fine for sketches or very small jobs.

# Variables

Now that we have a page that's doing what we want and looking the way we want, we can begin to replace static elements with programmatic elements using Handlebars. Let's start with our application's name. Let's say you want to localize the name of your application, showing "Rock Upprop" for your Swedish users, for instance. We'll need to do at least two things to make this work:

1. We'll need to use Handlebars to render a variable in place of our static HTML content.

2. We'll need to define that variable somewhere.

In practice, the definition of that variable could get quite involved. For now, let's just hang a variable on our RocknrollcallYeoman object. Speaking of, let's see what Java-Script was given to us by Yeoman in our *app/scripts/app.js* file:

```
var RocknrollcallYeoman = window.RocknrollcallYeoman = Ember.Application.cre
ate();

/* Order and include as you please. */
require('scripts/controllers/*');
require('scripts/store');
require('scripts/models/*');
require('scripts/routes/*');
require('scripts/views/*');
require('scripts/router');
```

Let's add a line, after the line in which we call `Ember.Application.create()`, that looks like this:

```
RocknrollcallYeoman.applicationName = "Rock'n'Roll Call";
```

See the change in this commit (*http://bit.ly/1loBG5R*).

In the future, we can add some fancy functionality that sets this variable to a localized version in any languages we wish to support. For the time being, this does mean that if we decided to change the name of our application, as long as we use Handlebars helpers every place we want to display the application's name, we'd only have to make that change in one place.

So, back to our template. Now we can simply change this line:

```
<a href="#" class="navbar-brand">Rock'n'Roll Call</a>
```

to this:

```
<a href="#" class="navbar-brand">{{RocknrollcallYeoman.applicationName}}</a>
```

See the change in this commit (*http://bit.ly/1k3NSVC*).

As we have seen before, this doesn't just inject your variable when the page is loaded. If `RocknrollcallYeoman.applicationName` were to change while the user was using your application—if, for instance, the user chose a different language from a preferences drop-down—that anchor tag's contents would be updated, automatically, without you having to write any more code than what we've written.

## Linking with the {{link-to}} Helper

While we're at it, that dummy link should be easy enough to actually hook up. We'll probably want clicking on the logo to take you back to the default state of the application, as though you'd just arrived. We haven't created any routes or controllers, yet, but, keep in mind, that doesn't mean that Ember hasn't. The page we're currently looking at in our browser is the... did you guess it? It's the default `IndexRoute`, nestled within the default `ApplicationRoute`. From here, our user will type in some search terms and hit Enter or click Play, either of which will take him to a search results route. Or he could click Activity to see a visualization of his search activity, which would take him to `ActivityRoute`. So, if he wanted to come back to this page we're looking at now, he would want to return to the `IndexRoute`. Well, that's easy enough. Replace that anchor tag with a Handlebars `link-to`, like so:

Static HTML:

```
<a href="#" class="navbar-brand">{{RocknrollcallYeoman.applicationName}}</a>
```

becomes the Handlebars template:

```
{{#link-to "index" class="navbar-brand"}}{{RocknrollcallYeoman.applicationName}}
{{/link-to}}
```

See the change in this commit (*http://bit.ly/1rEJxOJ*).

You're probably picking up on most of how this syntax works. The {{ and }} bits basically replace HTML's < and >. Like the opening an closing anchor tag in HTML, the link-to requires and opening tag—{{#link-to …}}—and a closing tag—{{/link-to}}. Inside that opening tag, just as with HTML, you can declare attributes of the anchor tag that will actually be rendered to the page, as we did in this example by declaring the classname of navbar-brand. The part you might be wondering about is that string right before that classname declaration: "index". Whereas with an HTML anchor you declare your target with an href attribute, with the Handlebars link-to helper, you pass a route, by name, as the first parameter. The naming convention is simple, once you get the hang of it. You take the camelcase version of your route's name (IndexRoute, in this case), remove Route, insert a hyphen before any capital letter but the first, separate the words if there are more than one, and make all the letters lowercase. That sounds complicated, written out that way, but visually it makes sense. Let's do a couple:

- Declaration name IndexRoute would be passed to a link-to as index.
- Declaration name SearchResultsRoute would be passed to a link-to as search-results.

You can read all about Ember's naming conventions at Ember Guides: Naming Conventions (*http://emberjs.com/guides/concepts/naming-conventions/*).

# Input with the {{input}} Helper

As you can imagine, the contents of that search input are going to become pretty important.input field as it is—accessing its value and intercepting its submit even with JavaScript—but it's far easier to let Handlebars and Ember do their thing. Let's replace our input tag with a Handlebars input helper:

Static HTML:

```
<input class="search-input" placeholder="Search for artists or song names">
```

becomes the Handlebars template:

```
{{input type="text" class="search-input" placeholder="Search for artists or
song names"}}
```

See the change in this commit (*http://bit.ly/1fpeCUy*).

As it is there, that input isn't going to do much. We'll look at binding its value and its submit event in the next chapter.

Let's turn our attention to search results. Here's the static HTML mockup we came up with:

```
<div class="container-fluid">
  <div class="row-fluid">
    <div class="search-results-wrapper clearfix">
      <div class="search-facets col-md-2">
        <h3>Show:</h3>
        <ul class="facets">
          <li>
            <label>Artists</label>
            <input type="checkbox" checked="checked">
          </li>
          <li>
            <label>Songs</label>
            <input type="checkbox" checked="checked">
          </li>
        </ul>
      </div>

      <div class="results col-md-10">
        <h3>Artists</h3>
        <ul class="search-results artists">
          <li><a href="#">Tom Waits</a></li>
          <li><a href="#">Tom Waits w; Keith Richards</a></li>
          <li><a href="#">Tom Waits/Keith Richards</a></li>
          <li><a href="#">Tom Waits [Vocalist] &amp; Orchestra [Orchestra]
            &amp; Michael Riesman [Conductor] &amp; Bryars, Gavin
            [Composer]</a></li>
          <li><a href="#">Tom Waits [Vocals] &amp; Gavin Bryars Ensemble
            [Ensemble]</a></li>
          <li><a href="#">Tom Waits [Vocalist]; Orchestra [Orchestra];
            Michael Riesman [Conductor]</a></li>
          <li><a href="#">Tom Waits [Vocals] &amp; Gavin Bryars Ensemble
            [Ensemble] &amp; Bryars, Gavin [Composer]</a></li>
          <li><a href="#">Tom Waits [Vocalist], Orchestra [Orchestra] &amp;
            Michael Riesman [Conductor]</a></li>
        </ul>

        <h3>Songs</h3>
        <ul class="search-results songs">
          <li><a href="#">"Tom Waits," by Panic Strikes a Chord</a></li>
          <li><a href="#">"Tom Waits," by Doug Kuony</a></li>
          <li><a href="#">"Tom Waits," by The Moonband</a></li>
          <li><a href="#">"Tom Waits," by The Moonband</a></li>
          <li><a href="#">"Tom Waits," by Spaghetti Western</a></li>
          <li><a href="#">"Tom Waits," by The Passionate &amp; Objective
            Jokerfan</a></li>
          <li><a href="#">"Tom Waits," by Mike Macharyas</a></li>
          <li><a href="#">"Tom Waits," by Junkyard Poets</a></li>
          <li><a href="#">"Tom Waits," by The Fall of Troy</a></li>
          <li><a href="#">"Tom Waits," by Anouk</a></li>
```

```
        </ul>
      </div>
    </div>
  </div>
</div>
```

For now, we wil add these results to *index.hbs*. We also need to add in a {{outlet}} to tell Ember where to render the template associated with the current route (index).

Figure 4-2 shows what the site looks like at the moment.

*Figure 4-2. Our search results template, rendered*

### But What Is This {{outlet}}, IndexRoute, and index.hbs?

We haven't covered how to get back and forth from one template to another. So for now, just know that we are rendering the content associated with the IndexRoute and *index.hbs* template into the {{outlet}} of *application.hbs*. Later, in the next chapter, we'll cover generating new templates, routes, and hooking everything up!

See the change in this commit (*http://bit.ly/1mR75Oa*).

# Lists with the {{each}} Helper

The first thing that might jump out at you as something inherently template-worthy might be those unordered lists. Handlebars has a nifty little helper for just such a thing. Let's reduce each of those lists to one item each, first, and then look at how to use the helper to replicate that template for each item we get back in our search results. So, here's the HTML version of the artists list:

```
<ul class="search-results artists">
        <li><a href="#">Tom Waits</a></li>
</ul>
```

In the end, we'll want one ul tag, just like that one, but we'll want potentially lots of li tags within it. Handlebars has an each helper that will iterate over an array, rendering a sort of inner template for each item in the array. So let's first create a dummy array object we can render. Add this line to *app.js*, just below our applicationName declaration:

```
RocknrollcallYeoman.dummySearchResultsArtists = [
  {
    id: 1,
    name: 'Tom Waits',
    nickname: 'Tommy',
    type: 'artist',
    enid: 'ARERLPG1187FB3BB39'
  },
  {
    id: 2,
    name: 'Thomas Alan Waits',
    type: 'artist',
    enid: 'ARERLPG1187FB3BB39'
  },
  {
    id: 3,
    name: 'Tom Waits w/ Keith Richards',
    type: 'artist',
    enid: 'ARMPVNN13CA39CF8FC'
  }
];
```

See the change in this commit (*http://bit.ly/QPTb3T*).

Now we can iterate over that array in our template. Replace that lonely little li tag with a helper, like so:

```
<ul class="search-results artists">
  {{#each RocknrollcallYeoman.dummySearchResultsArtists}}
    <li><a href="#">{{name}}</a></li>
  {{/each}}
</ul>
```

See the change in this commit (*http://bit.ly/1nVL8NG*).

Magical, isn't it? It's one thing that this helper is looping over our global variable. Like so much of Ember and Handlebars, the really magical part comes when the variable you passed—in our case, the global `dummySearchResultsArtists`—changes, and your list updates automatically.

Notice that the context—or variable scope—changes within the each helper. The text node within our anchor tag is referenced simply with `\{{name}}`, not `App.dummySear chResultsArtists[index].name` or anything of the like. Within the each loop, the context is set to the current object found within the array, and you can access its named properties by simply naming them.

What if we had a `nicknames` property on each of our `dummySearchResultsArtists` objects, which was an array of nicknames the artist had used. Suppose we wanted to display each of those nicknames as its own search result, so that "TAFKAP"—"The Artist Formerly Known as Prince"—would be its own search result. And to reduce confusion, we'll include "AKA: [real name, or original stage name here]." Someone might be searching for someone by a nickname and not even know it's only a nickname, after all.

You're probably thinking, because you're so clever, that our context switching might not be so convenient in this scenario. Let's take a look at why. Here's a first stab at this theoretical template (we'd really do it, but The Echo Nest doesn't supply nicknames):

```
<ul class="search-results artists">
  {{#each RocknrollcallYeoman.dummySearchResultsArtists}}
    {{#each ...
```

Oh, right! What do we call our local object? Well, you won't do this often, if ever, in practice, but it turns out, you can call it `this`:

```
<ul class="search-results artists">
  {{#each RocknrollcallYeoman.dummySearchResultsArtists}}
    <li><a href="#">{{this.name}}, AKA "{{this.nickname}}"</a></li>
  {{/each}}
</ul>
```

But, using `this` here just doesn't seem right, so fortunately Handlebars has us covered with another syntax for the each helper that lets you name your iterated variable, like so:

```
<ul class="search-results artists">
  {{#each artist in RocknrollcallYeoman.dummySearchResultsArtists}}
      <li><a href="#">{{artist.nickname}}, AKA "{{artist.name}}"</a></li>
  {{/each}}
</ul>
```

And, if you want to remove even more characters and simplify further, we don't even have to use this or a variable name. By convention, Handlebars will make the assumption that the current model object in the interated array is the current context:

```
<ul class="search-results artists">
  {{#each RocknrollcallYeoman.dummySearchResultsArtists}}
      <li><a href="#">{{nickname}}, AKA "{{name}}"</a></li>
  {{/each}}
</ul>
```

But now we've run into a different issue. Our artists with nicknames are rendering beautifully, but our artists without nicknames aren't rendering at all. This makes perfect sense, looking at our code. If you didn't have an array called nicknames, you would bypass that portion of the code altogether. We need something like an if statement. And, it may not surprise you at this point, Handlebars has this handled.

# Conditionals with the {{if}} and {{else}} Helpers

Let's check to see if the current artist has any nicknames first and then choose to loop over them or use a simpler template. That might look something like this:

```
<ul class="search-results artists">
  {{#each RocknrollcallYeoman.dummySearchResultsArtists}}
    {{#if nickname}}
        <li><a href="#">{{nickname}}, AKA "{{name}}"</a></li>
    {{else}}
      <li><a href="#">{{name}}</a></li>
    {{/if}}
  {{/each}}
</ul>
```

Figure 4-3 shows what the site looks like at the moment.

See the change in this commit (*http://bit.ly/1hHprQy*).

You may be wondering what's required of the nicknames attribute to evaluate as false. We would all expect the usual suspects to qualify, if assigned to that attribute in our data: false, null, undefined. But what if there was an empty array: [ ]? Handlebars evaluates all of those as false, rest assured.

Now we can remove the nickname logic, as it was purely for demonstration purposes. It won't really be supported, once we hook up to the real Echo Nest API service.

See the change in this commit (*http://bit.ly/QjkzpY*).

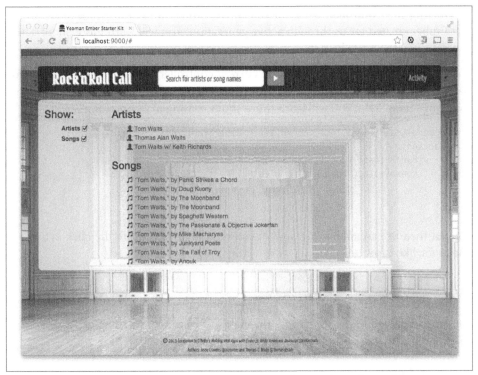

*Figure 4-3. Our search results template with dummy data and conditional logic, rendered*

# Capturing User Interaction with the {{action}} Helper

The {{action}} helper is available to capture events as the user interacts with your application. The action will bubble up to the controller that is associated with the current route. This will make more sense later once we have fully covered routes, but from your introduction in Chapter 2, you should at least be familiar with the basics.

The most common use case is to use an action to capture click events on an anchor tag or a button:

```
<button {{action 'doSomething'}}>CLICK ME!</button>
```

In order to handle this action, we need somewhere to handle the action. So let's create an IndexController by creating *app/scripts/controllers/index_controller.js*:

```
RocknrollcallYeoman.IndexController = Ember.Controller.extend({});
```

See the change in this commit (*http://bit.ly/1g1Jmew*).

By creating this controller, we are actually overriding an exisiting `IndexController` that Ember created for us through active generation. You will learn more about active generation in the next chapter.

You can now handle this action on the current controller, which is the `IndexControl ler` we just created, because we are hitting root URL (*http://localhost:3000/*). If that's confusing, hang tight; you will learn more about routing in Chapter 5:

```
RocknrollcallYeoman.IndexController = Ember.Controller.extend({
  actions: {
    viewedArtist: function(artist) {
      console.log('hang on I"m viewing: ' + artist.name)
    }
  }
});
```

We can then use an anchor tag and a custom actions to capture the click activity of our users, like this:

```
<li><a {{action 'viewedArtist' this }}>{{name}}</a></li>
```

See the change in this commit (*http://bit.ly/1mRfxzx*).

For more details on how we handle the action, stay tuned. In Chapter 7, we go into detail on how to persist this activity data locally and remotely.

## Bound Attributes

Continuing down our happy path, let's say the user clicks on an artist's name in those search results and is taken to an entity page. Later, in the next chapter, you'll learn how to create this new route, or application state, and navigate to it. For now, we'll look at the final template first and then dissect what we see. Add the following to *app/templates/artist.hbs*:

```
<div class="entity-artist page-container">
  <div class="artist-bio-lockup clearfix">
    {{#if model.image}}
      {{#if model.license}}
        {{#if model.license.url}}
          <a {{bind-attr href="model.license.url"}}>
            <img {{bind-attr src="model.image.url"}} class="pull-right">
          </a>
        {{else}}
          <img {{bind-attr src="model.image.url"}} class="pull-right">
        {{/if}}
      {{else}}
        <img {{bind-attr src="model.image.url"}} class="pull-right">
      {{/if}}
    {{/if}}
    <h3 class="fancy">{{model.name}}</h3>
    <h4>
```

```
      {{hotttnesss-badge model.hotttnesss}}
    </h4>
    <p class="bio pull-left">Biography(from {{model.biography.site}}):
    {{model.biography.text}}</p>
    <a {{bind-attr href="model.biography.url"}} class="pull-left">Read more</a>
  </div>

  {{#if model.videos.length}}
  <div class="videos">
    <h5>Videos</h5>
    {{#each video in videos}}
          <a {{bind-attr  href="video.url"}}><img  {{bind-attr  src="video.im
age_url"}} class="video-thumbnail"></a>
    {{/each}}
  </div>
  {{/if}}
</div>
```

See the change in this commit (*http://bit.ly/TAHLlt*).

Look over that block of code a few times. Guess what? There's only one new Ember concept in there. That new concept is expressed in the template as `bind-attr` attributes, which you'll see are inside curly braces and found *inside* HTML tags, where you'd normally find attributes declared. That's because they get rendered as attributes, eventually. The `bind-attr` directive allows you to dynamically assign any HTML attribute you like from any variable available in your context at runtime—most often from your model, but it could be something generated by a controller, view, or route.

The syntax is pretty simple. It's not a tag, so there's no opening and closing and therefore no need for a hash sign or a closing forward slash sign. You simply declare:

```
<[some tag] {{bind-attr }}>
```

Then you name the attribute you wish to populate—in this case, let's create a working link:

```
<a {{bind-attr href=video.url}}>Watch now on Vimeo</a>
```

Looking back at our template, you'll see plenty of examples of populating `href` attributes, `src` attributes of images, and one example of a `data-` attribute. You can bind to any attribute you like, including the `class` attribute. The `class` attribute, though, is a bit trickier, as you'll often have more than one, and each of them will need to be bound to different inputs. Handlebars offers a number of nifty tricks to handle lots of combinations of dynamic and static classname bindings, all detailed in this entry in the Ember.js guides, "Binding Element Class Names" (*http://bit.ly/1oe02gD*).

Now let's take a look at how we can create our own helper to refactor the code that we used earlier to display a hotttnesss badge.

# Creating Custom Helpers

So far, we have looked at helpers that are already included in Ember.js, such as the input Handlebars helper. The input helper is actually included in the Ember.js library as an extension to Handlebars. In fact, here it is, at the time of writing, on line 31514 in Ember.js 1.4.1+pre.af87bd20:

```
Ember.Handlebars.registerHelper('input', function(options) {
  Ember.assert('You can only pass attributes to the `input` helper,
  not arguments',
    arguments.length < 2);

  var hash = options.hash,
      types = options.hashTypes,
      inputType = hash.type,
      onEvent = hash.on;

  delete hash.type;
  delete hash.on;

  if (inputType === 'checkbox') {
    return Ember.Handlebars.helpers.view.call(this, Ember.Checkbox, options);
  } else {
    if (inputType) { hash.type = inputType; }
    hash.onEvent = onEvent || 'enter';
    return Ember.Handlebars.helpers.view.call(this, Ember.TextField, options);
  }
});
```

The cool thing is we can build our own custom Handlebars helpers, following this same pattern provided as an extension point by Handlebars. To demonstrate this, let's build a hotttnesss badge that displays flames and a number based on the hotttnesss property on our model.

If we were to do this without a helper, we would need to add multiple icon elements to *app/templates/index.hbs*, like this:

```
<h4>
  Hotness:
  {{#if model.hotttnesss}}
    <i class="hotttnesss">
      <i class="glyphicon glyphicon-fire hotttnesss0"></i>
      <i class="glyphicon glyphicon-fire hotttnesss1"></i>
      <i class="glyphicon glyphicon-fire hotttnesss2"></i>
      <i class="glyphicon glyphicon-fire hotttnesss3"></i>
      <i class="glyphicon glyphicon-fire hotttnesss4"></i>
      <i class="glyphicon glyphicon-fire hotttnesss5"></i>
      <i class="glyphicon glyphicon-fire hotttnesss6"></i>
      <i class="glyphicon glyphicon-fire hotttnesss7"></i>
      <i class="glyphicon glyphicon-fire hotttnesss8"></i>
      <i class="glyphicon glyphicon-fire hotttnesss9"></i>
```

```
    </i>
    <span class="hotttnesss-badge" {{bindAttr data-hotttnesss=
    "model.hotttnesss"}}></span>
  {{/if}}
</h4>
```

We would also need to create a style for each of those icon elements, such as the following for hotttnesss0:

```
h4 .hotttnesss .hotttnesss0 {
  font-size: 190%;
  top: -45%;
  left: -45%;
  position: absolute;
  color: #FF0000;
  direction: rtl;
  unicode-bidi: bidi-override;
}
```

So, instead of including all 10 *i* elements in the markup, we can write a helper that will include the markup based on the length of the model. We do this by converting the hotttness property that is stored as a value from between 0 and 1 to a value between 1 and 10, iterating over that value, dynamically creating the HTML, and outputting it:

```
Ember.Handlebars.helper('hotttnesss-badge', function(value, options) {
  var h = parseFloat(value);
  var hotttnesss_num = Math.round(h * 100);
  var hotttnesss_css = Math.ceil(h * 10) - 1;
  var html = "<h4>Hotness: ";
  if (hotttnesss_num > 0) {
    html += '<i class="hotttnesss">';
    for (var i=0;i<hotttnesss_css;i++) {
      html += '<i class="glyphicon glyphicon-fire hotttnesss'+i+'"></i>';
    }
    html += "</i>";
    html += '<span class="hotttnesss-badge">'+hotttnesss_num+'</span></h4>';
  } else {
    html += "0</h4>";
  }
  return new Handlebars.SafeString(html);
});
```

And finally, we need to add the hotttnesss property to our dummy data in *app/scripts/app.js*:

```
RocknrollcallYeoman.dummySearchResultsArtists = [
  {
    id: 1,
    name: 'Tom Waits',
    type: 'artist',
    enid: 'ARERLPG1187FB3BB39',
    hotttnesss: '1'
```

```
    },
    {
      id: 2,
      name: 'Thomas Alan Waits',
      type: 'artist',
      enid: 'ARERLPG1187FB3BB39',
      hotttnesss: '.89'
    },
    {
      id: 3,
      name: 'Tom Waits w/ Keith Richards',
      type: 'artist',
      enid: 'ARMPVNN13CA39CF8FC',
      hotttnesss: '.79'
    }
  ];
```

Now we can just add the helper in the template and pass in the data as the first parameter through the model like so:

```
{{hotttnesss-badge model.hotttnesss}}
```

See the change in this commit (*http://bit.ly/1sdz7DT*).

Figure 4-4 shows what the site looks like at the moment.

And, there you have it. Not only are we creating only the markup needed, we are also
simplifying our template to a single helper declaration.

This detailed information is better suited for a detail or entity view that we can navigate to in order to get more information on the particular search result. In the next
chapter, we will be setting up those views, so we will move the hotttnesss-badge to the
Song and Artist entity pages. Stay tuned!

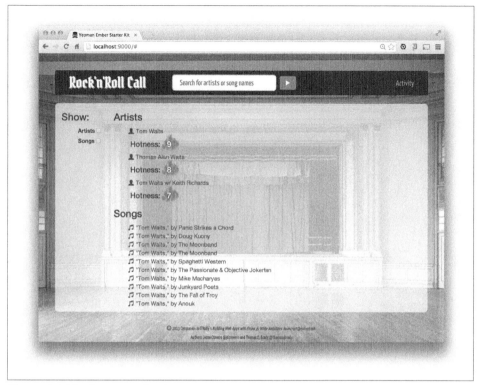

*Figure 4-4. The hotttnesss badge*

# Wrapping Things Up

Take a break for a minute and think about what we've done so far. We've written the vast majority of the markup for our site and even written a lot of it in such a way that it's dynamically rendered, injection-model data, conditionally rendering portions of our template and even iterating over arrays in our models.

Think, again, about the kind of work we've been doing. For the most part, an unskilled team member could have contributed a lot so far. Anyone who can edit HTML could have done the majority of this work, and with a little bit of investment on your part to teach them the concepts of variables, bound attributes, and conditionals, they could quite possibly do all of the kind of work we covered in this chapter without you. That's powerful, isn't it?

With that covered, let's move on to what you could be concentrating on while you're enlisting interns to input all your markup. The *real* models have to be created, and their data has to be funneled through these templates at some point. In Chapter 5, we will explore the router and basic models to see how.

# Building the RocknRollCall Prototype: The Router, Routes, and Models

If we set out to build a "single-page application," we've sure nailed that so far. But if we want our application to actually *do* anything, we're going to need to represent a few different application states, or what used to be described as "pages." In modern web applications, it should still mean a change to the value in your browser's address bar, most of the time.

For a few years now, HTML5's History API has made it possible—or at least far easier—to change the URL without reloading the page. What has not been so easy, without frameworks like Backbone.js and its kin, has been using that URL as a convenient way to serialize the state of your application. Serializing application state has always been tricky. Giving the user an easily portable token that both represents state in a high-resolution manner *and* is meaningful has been largely unheard of. The URL that you expose to your users is just such a token. They can bookmark it, send it to their mobile phone/tablet/refrigerator/friend and even tweet it. Consider Google Chrome, which uses URLs to grant access to its own settings panel. If a family member using Google Chrome asks you where they can disable cookies, you can send a link to that pane in the settings interface. Good luck doing the same with a native application.

Ember's Routing mechanisms offer a robust toolkit for building a complex matrix of states, and their APIs and conventions offer convenient ways to implement those states as routes. Ember's Controller APIs and conventions offer a similarly robust and convenient way to express application logic, interact with models, shuttle events back and forth among views and controllers, and quite often, navigate from route to route.

This is going to be a big chapter. We're going to map out the functionality of our site in terms of URLs, implement a router that organizes those URLs into a tree, create route classes that can serialize and deserialize state data in our models, and hand the data off to controllers. We'll look at the router, routes, and models, and before we're all done, our application will actually be able to see our application in several states, even if we can't use the application to navigate among them, quite yet.

**Yehuda Katz on URLs**

For an overall awesome talk on Ember and a great case made for thinking hard about URLs, check out Yehuda Katz's "Building Web Applications with Ember.js" (*http://bit.ly/1qRdgnu*) (starting at about 13:00) from HTML5DevConf 2013.

# URLs : The Web :: "Saved Game Passwords" : The Nintendo Entertainment System

If your childhood didn't involve feverishly copying "saved game passwords" by hand, straining your eyes to decipher often poorly rendered text on television screens, if "up, up, down, down, left, right…" doesn't ring a bell, then serialization might be a new concept for you. *In our day*, there was no persistent storage available in gaming consoles, and to allow for the illusion of saved progress, game makers would generate unique alphanumeric "passwords," that, when deciphered by the game engine, detailed your current game state—everything from what level you were on to how many lives you had left. You played the game for a while, got an updated "password," and confidently shut down your console, knowing that entering that password at the start of your next session would allow you to pick up where you left off.

This is *serialization* and *de-serialization*, in software terms. Serialization is the act of converting data into a format more ideal for long-term storage or transmission, usually a less verbose format that takes up less space on a disk or when transmitted across a wire. Most commonly, as in the case of the difficult-to-transcribe "saved game passwords," the serialized version of the data is not human readable. Most of the time this does not matter, as the serialized version of data is not exposed to the user. Web applications have a unique serialization/de-serialization mechanism that not only exposes serialized data to the user, but offers serialized data that is quite readable. The URL is that mechanism. Originally created as way to locate whole documents, modern server technologies have abstracted the URL to allow for arbitrary use—you, the developer, can choose to use the URL to locate a file by specifying a traditional file path or to serialize, in any way you see fit, your application's state data. When a user accesses your site via a URL—whether by clicking a link, opening her own bookmark, or typing it in manually—it's just like a player putting in her saved game password. The serialized data in your URL tells your application how to restore itself to the state in which the user left it, when she captured the URL. It's up to you to decide which bits of state are persisted and how to translate them into a URL (or serialize them), but Ember is going to make it pretty easy.

The great thing about the URL being visible to the user is that it has shamed developers into working hard to make the serialized version of the state data attractive, readable and even memorable. If you do recall the days of "saved game passwords," you almost assuredly remember the Metroid password "JUSTIN BAILEY." This was not the greatest Metroid password available—we used to get them from magazines and bulletin-board systems (BBSs), *in our day*, but it was far easier to remember than the random-number-and-letter combinations the game normally generated. Even "Narpas Sword," another popular password, was technically a "better" password, offering the player more progress and more inventory. I think "Justin Bailey" won the popularity contest because it's so much easier to remember. It's a proper noun. If you hear it, you can type it out. Even if you're not sure of the spelling, you know a few different spellings you can try. This makes for a *great* serialized state token, one that I remember clearly 25—I mean, 15—years later.

Great web applications include carefully crafted URLs, putting frequently used application states a short keystroke or bookmark click away. If you use Twitter, you probably know that you can see a user's timeline by navigating to *http://twitter.com/[USER-NAME]*. Less awesome applications obscure things, with needless obfuscation, à la Google+ URLs, like mine (Figure 5-1), or careless construction, such as the easily forgotten */in/* that disappears into the middle of a LinkedIn profile URL, like mine (Figure 5-2).

*Figure 5-1. I give it a Google–*

*Figure 5-2. /in/? More like easily left /out/*

# Routing

All this time, we've thrown the word *router* around as though we all know we're using it the same way. If you haven't encountered that word in similar usage, perhaps when learning or using another MVC framework, it is pretty much what it sounds like. A router is a logical mechanism that routes things.

You can send that fan mail to *tqb@thomasqbrady.com*.

OK, but seriously, folks, just like the person at your local post office who has "router" in his title, our version of a router routes packages to the right places. A request comes in—the mailperson is asked to deliver a package and our router is asked to deliver a route, which includes the right model(s), view(s), controller(s), and template(s)

—to the router, and a response—the mailperson drops a package into the right bin, our router finds and returns the right route—is sent.

Routing, in Ember, is handled in two pieces. First, you need a map. Just as the mailperson compares the address on a package and their maps of which neighborhoods belong to which zip codes, our router will match a URL to our model, view, controller, and template bundle. Remember that potentially complex matrix we mentioned a few paragraphs back? It doesn't always have to be that complex, but it does have to map every URL to which you want your app to respond. If you're coming from a backend-development background, this is not so different from mapping out your application by starting with your API. The next step is to restore the application state, with all of the pieces we've retrieved, and any encoded data that may have also been sent along, exactly like our "saved game password." Ember lets you define this map with a class method on `Ember.Router` called—you guessed it—`map`. We'll take a look in a just a second.

Second, we'll need the thing that our map helps us find to enable us to rebuild our application to the desired state. That thing, the thing that our map will help us find, is a `route`. We'll take a look at how routes manage state, including serilizaion/deserialization, after we've figured out our map.

**Keeping an Eye on and Debugging Routes in the Console**

Before things get going, there's a useful logging feature we can enable that will help illustrate what's going on. It's also a lifesaver for debugging route issues. Add this object as a parameter passed when we instantiate our Ember application on line 1 in *app/scripts/app.js*:

```
var RocknrollcallYeoman = window.RocknrollcallYeoman =
Ember.Application.create({
  LOG_TRANSITIONS: true
});
```

See the change in this commit (*http://bit.ly/1jsfs2K*).

Now every time you change routes in your appliation, Ember will write out a helpful debug statement to the console (Figure 5-3).

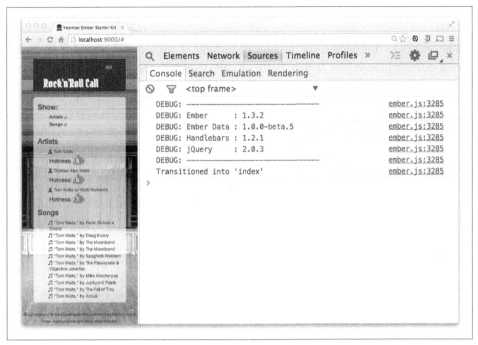

*Figure 5-3. Logging router transitions*

## The Router

Let's build a map. While we're on that topic, why have we gotten so far without one? Let's not forget that we get some things for free with Ember. Ember has been very politely creating default maps and routes for us. Even after we define our own, we'll still make frequent use of Ember's conventions, and not having to specifically declare the names of and paths to our definitions of all of our views, controllers, and templates. Ember will assume that it can find all of those things based on what we named our routes. Assuming we stick with convention, we get to save a lot of typing.

The domain name of our app—currently *http://localhost:9000*—won't really matter. Ember won't care if that part changes. Everything after that, though, will matter. Even with nothing specified there, you're hitting a default route: the IndexRoute. When your user navigates to *http://localhost:9000/#/search/tom waits*, the */search* and */tom waits* parts will be given significance and will be translated into a route in the former case and de-serialized to state data in the latter case.

So, what do we currently have? We already have an ApplicationRoute:

```
RocknrollcallYeoman.ApplicationRoute = Ember.Route.extend({
    model: function () {
        return ['red', 'yellow', 'blue'];
```

```
    }
  });
```

We haven't used this code since the very beginning of our journey, when we first generated our applicaton in Chapter 3, so we can go ahead and delete it. The `Applica tionRoute` is entered when the application is first initialized, primarily to render the application template; it isn't often we would use it in an evolved application. It will be generated for us if we dont have it explicitly created.

See the change in this commit (*http://bit.ly/1oBkryj*).

We also have an `IndexRoute`. In Chapter 4, we briefly introduced the *index.hbs* template. Behind the scenes, Ember generated an `IndexRoute` for us. You may be beginning to see that this is one of the magical features of Ember, called active generation.

### Understanding Active Generation

When Ember doesn't find a route handler or a controller, it will actively generate one. This is one of the most frustrating aspects of Ember for newcomers. But once you undersand and embrace it, you'll see that it can be a huge timesaver to only have to write code when you need to. We can turn on logging of this feature, within our `Application.create()` configuration object:

```
var RocknrollcallYeoman = window.RocknrollcallYeoman =
Ember.Application.create({
  LOG_TRANSITIONS: true,
  LOG_ACTIVE_GENERATION: true
});
```

See the change in this commit (*http://bit.ly/1nse2YR*).

Now in our console we can see the active generation of both the `ApplicationControl ler` and the `IndexRoute` (Figure 5-4).

*Figure 5-4. Logging active generation*

OK, so now that we know what we have and what is being created for us, let's start making our own routes. Once the user types in some search terms and hits Enter, we'll want to show search results, so we'll need a `SearchResultsRoute`. From there, our user will click on artists' names or song titles to view entity pages for each, so we'll need an `ArtistRoute` and a `SongRoute`.

Let's take a look at the current state of our *app/scripts/app.js*:

```
var RocknrollcallYeoman = window.RocknrollcallYeoman = Ember.Application.cre
ate({
  LOG_TRANSITIONS: true,
  LOG_ACTIVE_GENERATION: true
});

RocknrollcallYeoman.applicationName = "Rock'n'Roll Call";

RocknrollcallYeoman.dummySearchResultsArtists = [
  {
    id: 1,
    name: 'Tom Waits',
    type: 'artist',
    enid: 'ARERLPG1187FB3BB39',
    hotttnesss: '1'
  },
```

```
  {
    id: 2,
    name: 'Thomas Alan Waits',
    type: 'artist',
    enid: 'ARERLPG1187FB3BB39',
    hotttnesss: '.89'
  },
  {
    id: 3,
    name: 'Tom Waits w/ Keith Richards',
    type: 'artist',
    enid: 'ARMPVNN13CA39CF8FC',
    hotttnesss: '.79'
  }
];

/* Order and include as you please. */
require('scripts/controllers/*');
require('scripts/store');
require('scripts/models/*');
require('scripts/routes/*');
require('scripts/views/*');
require('scripts/router');
```

...

While we're here, let's go ahead and remove some cruft. You might want to go back and tinker with what we have so far, so feel free to comment out rather than delete, but let's get rid of our dummySearchResultsArtists object. We won't need these training wheels any longer.

See the change in this commit (*http://bit.ly/1jd3vJm*).

Now, let's take a look in *app/scripts/router.js*. Here's where we'll define all those routes we outlined a few paragraphs back. The map function takes a callback function as its argument; when that callback is called, it is passed a reference to your application's Router instance, in the variable this. In this callback, you will define all your application's routes. Typically you'll see this defined inline. Within that callback, you can call the route method on the Router instance assigned to this to create a route. Here are all the routes we've discussed so far, added to *app/scripts/router.js*:

```
RocknrollcallYeoman.Router.map(function() {
  this.route('search-results');
  this.route('artist');
  this.route('song');
});
```

See the change in this commit (*http://bit.ly/1hEhCrA*).

---

Notice we didn't define an `application` or `index` route, because, as we said, we get those for free. If we wanted to customize them somehow, we could define them here, but we're not doing anything interesting with them, at least not yet.

Remember how in Chapter 4 we put our search results HTML in *index.hbs*? We had to do that because we didn't have a way to get from our `IndexRoute` to the `SearchRe sultsRoute`. In fact, the `SearchResultsRoute` didn't even exist, yet. Later, we will be able to move that HTML into its proper template, *search-results.hbs*.

For now, we've told Ember that we want the user to be able to navigate to *http://local-host:9000/#/search-results*, *http://localhost:9000/#/artist*, and *http://localhost:9000/#/song*. We've declared that we want those `route` objects to exist, and therefore Ember will create default instances for us, even if we don't create our own.

**Convention over Configuration**

If the conventions for naming things in Ember are not clicking for you, or if you just want to learn more about how and why they work, look no further than the API documentation for Ember.De-faultResolver (*http://bit.ly/1qRcBT3*).

Pop quiz: what would happen if you pulled up *http://localhost:9000/#/search-results* in a browser right now, having not yet created a Handlebars template (or a route), yet? We'll get a page that contains our `application` template and what looks like an empty spot where our `search-results` template would go. Technically, it's only empty because the default `search-results` template that Ember created for us is empty. If you did guess that, then you have already understood what the router does, and why we wrote that `map` callback.

## Dynamic Routes

If you go and pull up those URLs now, you'll find they all *exist*. They're all supported. But they're not terribly useful, yet. You can begin to set up the templates for those pages and get some of the page structure—at least the markup and CSS—put in place, but even that's going to be tough because we haven't hooked up the user's search request yet. When you go to the `search-results` route, you can see the *search-results.hbs* template, but we can't populate the page with any data because we don't know who or what the user searched for yet. We'll probably want to reflect that in our URL, something like *http://localhost:9000/#/search-results/tom waits*. Try that URL out right now, and, if you have your console showing, you'll see an error message. Ember doesn't know where to go. We haven't defined a route that matches */search-results/tom waits*.

"Wait a minute," you might be saying, "how can I define a route for every possible thing the user might search for?" You're astute. The answer is you can't. And you shouldn't have to. And you don't have to. What we *do* need is a route with a "wild-card," what's called a *dynamic segment*.

This is way easier than it sounds. Let's start with the syntax to define the dynamic segment. In our `map` function, we can specify what we want our URL, or "path," to look like, including a dynamic portion, by passing an options object as the second argument, like this:

```
RocknrollcallYeoman.Router.map(function() {
  this.route('search-results', {
    path: 'search/:term'
  });
  this.route('artist');
  this.route('song');
});
```

The `:term` part is our dynamic segment. If you go to the URL *http://localhost:9000/#/ search/tom waits* now, you no longer get the error message about that route not existing. In a few paragraphs or so, we'll see that Ember has plucked out the part of the URL that matches up to this dynamic segment and made it available to your route.

We sneaked another feature in there while we were at it. Did you notice? We specified the path */search/:term*. This means our URL will read *http://localhost:9000// search/tom waits* instead of *http://localhost:9000//search-results/tom waits*. "Search-results" makes a better class name than it does a URL. Thanks to the `map` function, we can define separate strings for what shows in our URL and what we call our routes.

See the change in this commit (*http://bit.ly/1nsjdYJ*).

Speaking of routes, let's look at how those work.

# Routes

So, if we've used the `map` function to declare our routes, and Ember is now using those names to find our views, controllers, and templates, what's left? What else does a route need to do?

It makes intuitive sense that a URL and view can be so tightly coupled—that they would share a name, for instance. Continuing that line of reasoning, why wouldn't your template have the same name as your view? And, while we're at it, your controller? They're all parts of a team that is responsible for linking application logic, state, and a user interface. The only thing missing from this list is a model. Your models are not tied very directly to your routes, though. Your models are probably more persistent than particular routes; your models are probably used by more than one route.

This being the case, there must be some way to match up the required model(s) with a particular controller or view, right? Why, in fact, there is, and it's called a route!

We've most recently been getting data into our templates by making use of variables hung off the global App object so far, promising along the way that we'd fix that. When we first loaded the Ember start kit, way back in Chapter 2, we saw a glimpse of the right solution. In that example application, we made use of the model method defined in our IndexRoute to define a model. Whatever we returned from that method *became* the model, which we could then pluck properties from to populate our templates.

The model method is one of the biggest reasons you'll use Ember's Routes. One key feature of the model method is that it can be used to de-serialize your URL into model/state data. We left off, just a few paragraphs back, in the middle of talking about dynamic segments, having introduced them, but not really having covered what they're useful for. Here's what they're good for. We defined the route search-results with the path *search/:term*, and now if we visit the URL *http://localhost:9000/#/search/tom waits* in our application, our SearchResultsRoute will have an argument passed to its model method. That value of that argument will be... our dynamic segment! It will be "tom waits". This may not have you jumping out of your seat, just yet, but believe me, it's pretty convenient. You can imagine, no doubt, a few ways that you could take that argument and turn it into some useful data, such as would be required to populate a search-results page.

Our search-results route is going to have one slightly complicated aspect to it that we don't want to get tangled in, just yet, so let's set it aside for a moment and jump ahead in our application. When the user gets to this search-results route in our finished application, she'll click, assuming she's found what she was after, an artist's name or song title, which will be rendered by a linkTo helper. That link will then transition her to either the artist or the song route. We're going to have the same issue with those that we had with search-results: we will need a dynamic segment in order to support a myriad of artists and songs with just two routes.

Right, back to the map! Let's add some dynamism to those routes:

```
RocknrollcallYeoman.Router.map(function() {
  this.route('search-results', {
    path: 'search/:term'
  });
  this.route('artist', {
    path: 'artist/:enid'
  });
  this.route('song', {
    path: 'song/:enid'
  });
});
```

See the change in this commit (*http://bit.ly/1ogyufq*).

"Who is Enid?" you might be asking. It's short for "Echo Nest ID," the unique ID assigned to each row in The Echo Nest's database. The search-results lists that we will get back from Echo Nest's search API will include these unique IDs, which we will then use to request further information about the selected artist or song, in order to populate an entity page.

So now we have routes for individual artists and songs. If a user were to get this far starting from scratch, they would now have a URL that looked like this, corresponding to Tom Waits' entity page: *http://localhost:9000/#/artist/ARERLPG1187FB3BB39*. That last bit is the Echo Nest ID, the dynamic segment for our `artist` route.

What are we going to do with that `enid`? We now know that our `model` method will get that string passed as an argument, giving us a chance to create a model object to be passed off to the `controller` to be used to populate our template, and so on, but how do we turn this very "saved game password"-esque "ARERLPG1187FB3BB39" into a model object?

This is a great opportunity to look at a real-world problem that we don't seem to find answered in many of the Ember training materials. How do you incorporate third-party services? Well, here's one way.

First, let's finally talk about models; and while we're at it, let's make one! Then, let's define an `ArtistRoute` class, with a `model` method, and within that method, let's make an XHR against The Echo Nest's API, passing our `enid` and using what Echo Nest sends back to us to create an instance of our fancy, new `Artist` model.

# Models

Until we get into persistence, you won't actually be using Ember's `Model` classes, and with good reason.  Models, as a concept, mostly exist for the purposes of persistence (by persistence, here, just so we're clear, we mean storing something in a database of some kind for long-term storage and retrieval). In our application, there's some transient data—data that we don't plan to store to a database—that would still probably do well to be kept in a model. For one thing, we *are* dealing with structured data, and models are good for defining such structures. For another, technically speaking, the data we're putting in these models *is* being persisted, on someone else's server (The Echo Nest).

There's a lower-level `Object` class that is actually a great fit for something like a proto-model, offering computed properties, data binding and convenient methods to extend the class. For our purposes, it will do. Let's define our "model":

```
RocknrollcallYeoman.Artist = Em.Object.extend({
  id: null,
```

```
    name: null,
    enid: null,
    biography: null,
    hotttnesss: null,
    image: null,
    videos: null
});
```

Notice that we extended Ember's Object class, and that we defined all of the properties our Artist class *could* have. We gave all of these properties a default value of null, but we could have given default strings, booleans, numbers, etc. to any or all of these properties.

See the change in this commit (*http://bit.ly/1jsiF2z*).

To instantiate an Artist, simply create an Artist, like so, passing an object containing the properties of an Artist that you wish to define:

```
var artist = RocknrollcallYeoman.Artist.create({
    enid: 'ARERLPG1187FB3BB39',
    name: 'Tom Waits',
    hotttnesss: 100,
    biography: 'Rain dog.',
    image: 'http://is.gd/GeaUhC'
});
```

Armed with our proto-model, let's jot down, in pseudocode, how we're going to instantiate one in our ArtistRoute's model method:

```
RocknrollcallYeoman.ArtistRoute = Ember.Route.extend({
    model: function(params) {
        /* pseudocode
        XHR("some URL",{"id":params.enid},function callback(response){
            var artist = App.Artist.create({
                name: response.name,
                hotttnesss: response.hotttnesss,
            });
        });
        */
    }
});
```

See the change in this commit (*http://bit.ly/1kVBBEf*).

If you're paying attention, there are at least two problems with that pseudocode, and failure to compile isn't one of them.

For one thing, we're not returning anything from the model method. Our route won't have anything to pass on to our controller, leaving our templates high and dry.

For another, how in the world *would* we return anything? We have a callback issue here. We can't return our artist object within the XHR callback, because we wouldn't be returning the object in the right scope. Within the right scope, how are we going to make sure we have gotten something back from our XHR before returning said object?

## Promises, Promises

You can't throw a rock at a JavaScript developer's blog without bouncing it off two articles about Promises, lately. Promises are a new feature in ES6 (EcmaScript 6, the latest version of JavaScript, at the time of this writing, so new it isn't fully supported in all modern browsers, yet) that offer a solution to our "when will everything be ready?" conundrum. For an in-depth explanation of the problem and the solution that Promises offer, I recommend the HTML5 Rocks article: "JavaScript Promises: There and Back Again" (*http://www.html5rocks.com/en/tutorials/es6/promises/*). In the all-too-recent old days, you might have tackled this chicken-and-egg problem by setting up a variable in the outermost scope meant to hold the model, once populated, setting up an XHR, whose success callback would populate that variable and then call yet another callback, with the assurance that the model variable was now populated and we can get on with the show.

As you can imagine, that sort of thing is even more tiring to author than it is to have just read about. What's worse, it still wouldn't solve our scope issue, of returning something immediately in the model method, that would, eventually, actually contain a model.

Promises offer a better, or at least far more convenient, way, that looks like this:

```
Promise.all([functionOnWhichWeDepend(), anotherFunctionOnWhichWeDepend(),
    yetAnotherFunctionOnWhichWeDepend()]).then(function() {
  console.log("They're all finished, success is ours!")
}, function() {
  console.error("One or more FAILED!")
});
```

That `all` method takes an array of methods, then returns a `Promise` object. That `Promise` object has a `then` method, which accepts two callbacks, one which will be called if every one of the methods passed in `all` has successfully returned something, and one to call if any of them fails. See how much shorter this paragraph was, let alone the actual code?

Now that we get the concept of promises, let's take a look at two specific implementations: the Ember core team's RSVP and a simple example in jQuery.

### RSVP

Ember bundles the popular library RSVP.js (created and maintained by a team of Ember core contributors), which provides an excellent implementation of the Promises specification, even in browsers that don't yet support Promises (which is more of them than you'd prefer). What's more, Ember mixes in Promises functionality to a lot of its core objects. For instance, our `model` method can return a `Promise` object, and, if it does, the router will be notified when the Promise is resolved. If you have default values in your models, those will be pushed into your templates and rendered to the screen, and then the router will wait for your model method's returned Promise to fulfill. If it does so successfully, your new model data will be pushed through, and your templates will be updated with the new data.

### Other Promise implementations

The only catch at the moment, regarding Promises, due to the fact that the specification is still so new, is that there are a few different "flavors" out there, each with slightly different APIs. It's not as bad as it sounds, but know that you will often be dealing with more than one flavor in an Ember project: RSVP, mentioned previously, and the version within jQuery. All jQuery AJAX calls (such as `getJSON`), for instance, return `Promise` objects, which we will see in the next example. No worries: the APIs should be, and in most cases are, so similar that you can use them almost interchangeably.

## The model() Method

Let's take a crack at that `model` method, now that we have a game plan. jQuery's `getJSON` will return a `Promise` object, so let's use that method to request data from the Echo Nest, returning that `Promise` object, which will, itself, return a newly minted `Artist` model. Here's how I did it:

```
RocknrollcallYeoman.ArtistRoute = Ember.Route.extend({
  model: function(params) {

    var url = "http://developer.echonest.com/api/v4/artist/profile?api_key
    =<YOUR-API-KEY>&format=json&bucket=biographies&bucket=blogs&bucket=
    familiarity&bucket=hotttnesss&bucket=images&bucket=news&bucket=reviews
    &bucket=terms&bucket=urls&bucket=video&bucket=id:musicbrainz",
      obj = {"id": params.enid};

    return Ember.$.getJSON(url, obj)
      .then(function(data) {
        var entry = data.response.artist;
        var bio = null;
        var img = null;
        for (i = 0;i<entry.biographies.length;i++) {
          if (entry.biographies[i].site.toLowerCase() == "wikipedia") {
            bio = entry.biographies[i];
          }
        }
        if (!bio && entry.biographies.length > 0) {
          bio = entry.biographies[0];
        }
        if (entry.images.length) {
```

```
        img = entry.images[0];
      }
      var lastVideo = 4;
      if (entry.video.length < 4) {
        lastVideo = entry.video.length;
      }
      var videos = [];
      for (i=0;i<lastVideo;i++) {
        videos.push(entry.video[i]);
      }

      return RocknrollcallYeoman.Artist.create({
        enid: entry.id,
        name: entry.name,
        hotttnesss: entry.hotttnesss,
        biography: bio,
        image: img,
        videos: videos
      });
    });
  },
});
```

Walking through that code, we:

1. Define a `model` method that accepts a `params` argument.

2. Define a `url` variable that is an Echo Nest API request, with numerous flags set to dial in the kind of data we want to get returned to us. You'll need your own API key, so see the aside about that.

3. Define an object, `obj`, in which we'll hold the request body and include the Echo Nest ID of the entity for which we want more data.

4. We then immediately return the `Promise` object returned from jQuery's (`Ember.$` is a shortcut to jQuery) `getJSON`.

   Keep in mind, `getJSON` *immediately* returns the `Promise` object, and later, when the Promise is broken or fulfilled, `then` will be called on that `Promise` object.

5. Chain a `then` method which, upon fulfillment of the Promise returned by the `getJSON` method, will be called and passed the response body of the XHR in an argument (`'data'`).

6. Then we do several things with that response data:

   a. We sift through the biographies, plucking either the first Wikipedia biography that we find or just using the first biography we find if we don't find a Wikipedia biography.

   b. Grab an image URL, if there is one.

   c. Grab up to four video URLs to embed, if there are any.

7. Finally, we create and return an `Artist` model and fill it with all the material we've just pulled out of the response body from The Echo Nest's API.

See the change in this commit (*http://bit.ly/1iBh45m*).

### Get Your Own Echo Nest API Key!

You'll need your own API key for The Echo Nest, but don't worry —it's a quick, easy process to get one. Just visit *https://develop er.echonest.com/account/register* in your browser, fill out the form, and follow the directions. Once you've activated your account, you'll land on your brand-new profile page, which will contain your API key, consumer key, and shared secret, as well as forms to allow you to change your profile info. The API key listed there is all you'll need for now.

# Wrapping Things Up

This is by far the most intimidating code we've written so far, but it breaks down pretty easily, doesn't it? We still have very little code, but we've got quite a bit of power already. We have a router that lets us easily respond to numerous URLs, with dynamic segments and custom path names, four custom routes, an `Artist` model, and an `ArtistRoute`, which can respond to a URL with an Echo Nest ID in it and can, using an XHR, turn that ID into a full-fledged `Artist` model. And along the way, we learned about Promises, and how they hold fast that potentially leaky connection between our route and our controllers. You guys! We are so close to a finished application! One more chapter and we'll have a working music search engine!

# Building the RocknRollCall Prototype: Controllers, Views, Data Binding, and Events

We've figured out templates. We've figured out routers and routes. We've figured out models. What's left?

Well, we need a place to keep track of moment-to-moment state data: the kind of stuff you absolutely need to know right now but you probably don't need to write to a database. This is the kind of state that you expect to reset when you leave and come back to a site. We also need a place for more complicated rendering logic. We need a way to coordinate this fancy renderer and our moment-to-moment state data manager.

For the transient state data, we need controllers. We need views for the extended rendering control. We need events to connect controllers and views, and, finally, we need data binding to keep our data in-sync across all these pieces.

When we've got all these in place, we'll have a working prototype. Let's do it!

## Controllers

Yes, you've gotten all the way to Chapter 6 in a book about an MVC framework without *really* talking about views or controllers (or really-real models, for that matter). Don't worry. You'll get your money's worth.

In Ember, controllers have these four most important jobs (among others):

- Manipulate the data within the application's models

- Store transient data, whether standalone or made up of data retrieved from models

- Listen to events dispatched by and dispatch events intended for other controllers, views, and templates

- Instigate the transition from one route to another

As you can see, this is critical stuff. Without controllers, your application wouldn't amount to much.

Backing up a bit in our application's development, we never made it possible to get from the `IndexRoute` to the `SearchResultsRoute`. Typing "Tom Waits" into the search box at the top of our application and hitting Enter doesn't *do* anything, yet. Let's fix that. Add this very simple `ApplicationController` to your *app.js*:

```
RocknrollcallYeoman.ApplicationController = Em.ObjectController.extend({
    searchTerms: '',
    applicationName: "Rock'n'Roll Call",
    actions: {
      submit: function() {
        this.transitionToRoute('search-results',this.get('searchTerms'));
      }
    }
});
```

Starting on the second line in the newest block of code, we've created a transient variable local to our controller called `searchTerms`, a real home for our application name (you can go ahead and delete the line in which we hung a variable of the same name off of the `App` global variable), followed by an `actions` object, which will be covered in a few paragraphs.

Also, we still have a leftover `IndexController` from a simple demonstration of `actions` in Chapter 4, so let's remove *app/scripts/controllers/index_controller.js* because we won't be using it.

See the changes in this commit (*http://bit.ly/1iBiU60*).

We can now plug in a reference to `searchTerms` in our template, just as we did with model data in previous chapters. Here's where we left the search section within our *application.hbs* template:

```
<ul class="nav navbar-nav search-lockup">
  <li class="search-group">
    {{input type="text" class="search-input" placeholder="Search for artists or
    song names"}}
    <button class="btn btn-primary"><i class="glyphicon glyphicon-play"></i>
    </button>
  </li>
</ul>
```

We've seen a couple examples of putting variables from models into the `text` node—the space between the opening and closing tags of a typical HTML element. In this case, though, we want to bind our variable to the `value` property of our `input` helper. The `input` allows its value to be bound via a `valueBinding` property on the helper, like so:

```
<li class="search-group">
  {{input class="search-input" placeholder="Search for artists or song names"
    valueBinding="controller.searchTerms"}}
  <button class="btn btn-primary"><i class="glyphicon glyphicon-play"></i>
  </button>
</li>
```

Notice that we declared `controller.searchTerms`. Had we not specified the controller was our source, Ember would have assumed it should find the `searchTerms` variable within the model, and, indeed, if there was *also* a variable by that name within the model, its value would have been injected into the template.

If you were to reload your application now, you would not be blown away, exactly. Although we *have* bound the value of the `input` and our `searchTerms` value, we're not *doing* anything with that value. We defined an `actions` block in our controller. Let's see how you reference an `action` from a template. It looks like this:

```
<li class="search-group">
  {{input action="submit" type="text" class="search-input" placeholder="Search
for artists or song names" valueBinding="controller.searchTerms"}}
  <button {{action "submit"}} class="btn btn-primary">
    <i class="glyphicon glyphicon-play"></i>
  </button>
</li>
```

We added two `action` references there, in case you didn't notice. Typically speaking, the `action` helper adds a "click" event listener to the element to which it is added. You could say adding an `action` to an element "makes it clickable." In the case of our Play button, that's exactly what we're looking for. The user should be able to type in a search term and click the Play button to search. In the case of our `Ember.TextField`, though, Ember knows you probably don't want to click your `input` tag to fire the event, but rather that the `submit` event of HTML forms is the one you're looking for. In most browsers, this is what happens if you type into the form element and hit Enter. This is the event to which Ember will bind an `action` reference within an `input` helper.

The `actions` object we defined within our controller defines event handlers for events fired by our templates. In our templates, we defined an `action` called "submit," so Ember fires a `submit` event when those elements are triggered (by click or by keystroke). Our controller then looks for a handler of matching name within its `actions` block and fires the handler.

Save the changes we've just made and reload your page. Type in a search term and click the Play button. It worked (hopefully!)! You've just navigated from one view to another!

See the change in this commit (*http://bit.ly/1max2J7*).

Following along with the code, it's not too hard to see the trail. In your *application.hbs* template you added an `action` attribute to the `button` tag. When the template was rendered, Ember, therefore, added a `click` handler to the `button`, which, when fired, looked for a handler called `submit` within the `actions` object in your controller and executed that handler. In our case, that handler used the `transitionToRoute` method of the `Ember.Controller` class, which tells (or *asks*) the `Router` to navigate to a new route—the one passed as the first argument to the `transitionToRoute` method.

Pay special attention to what we pass as that second argument: the search terms the user entered. That should be no surprise, but it *should* set your mind to wondering how what we pass there gets turned into the dynamic segment. You did notice that, right? Whatever is typed into the search box gets tacked onto the URL (of the new / *search* path) after you click the Play button. Give yourself a minute to ponder how that might be happening based on what you've read so far.

Did you guess it? This is serialization. The argument you pass to `transitionToRoute` is usually a model that you want to pass to the route, although it can be, and is, in this case, just a string. You have the opportunity, in your route, to define a `serialize` method that accepts what is passed in here, and turn it into a path string, which it returns. So, in other words, the `serialize` method takes data in and outputs a URL— it *serializes* the data. Sometimes, as in our case, the data that you're passing in the first place is already a string, the very string you want to use as your path—no transformation necessary.

We haven't written a `serialize` method, yet, though. How, then, is our application already serializing that argument?

Oh, right: "Because this pattern is so common, it is the default." If we don't define a `serialize` method of our own, the default implementation passes the argument right on through if it happens to already be a string.

While you have that template open, it would be a good time to swap out this line:

```
{{#link-to "index" class="navbar-brand"}}{{RocknrollcallYeoman.applicationName}}
{{/link-to}}
```

with this:

```
{{#link-to "index" class="navbar-brand"}}{{applicationName}}{{/link-to}}
```

This simply replaces our global variable anti-pattern with our `ApplicationControl
ler` reference to our application's name.

See the change in this commit (*http://bit.ly/1ldhfbe*) and this commit (*http://bit.ly/TAJiIg*).

# Computed Properties

Computed properties are one of the biggest selling points of Ember. In most training materials, they're one of the first concepts covered. We've saved it until now in hopes that the added context will make it easier to appreciate just how useful they are.

We've named our application "Rock'n'Roll Call," a play on the concept of roll call, wherein someone stands at the front of a room and rattles off names from a list, one by one, and attendees of whatever meeting is being called respond, "Present!" when their name is called. So, for a little moment of delight, let's have our site's name walk through this familiar interaction. When you first arrive at the site, let's have our application name proudly displayed. When you search for something, "Tom Waits," for instance, let's change that text to "Tom Waits???"

We can do all of that with a computed property. Let's do an easy one, first. Replace your `applicationName` variable in `App.ApplicationController` with this one:

```
applicationName: function() {
  var st = this.get('searchTerms');
  if (st) {
    return st + "???"
  } else {
    return "Rock'n'Roll Call"
  }
}.property('searchTerms'),
```

Let's start with the last line of that block: the `property` function that we call on what gets returned from `applicationName`. That `property` function takes the name of one or more properties on which your computed property (`applicationName`, in this case) should depend. We've specified here that `applicationName` depends on the property `searchTerms`, a property of our controller. You can specify properties of other objects—other controllers, models, etc. Because we've specified this dependency, Ember will now watch our `searchTerms` property for changes. Any time it changes, the function we've defined as our `applicationName` will be fired, returning a new value for our `applicationName` variable. In this example, if the `searchTerms` property has a truthy value, we return that and a few question marks, a la "Tom Waits???" If it has a falsy value, we return our application's name. Computed properties can exist on anything that extends `Ember.Object`, which includes controllers, models, and more. You can read all about computed properties at the source, Emberjs.com's Ember.ComputedProperty class API documentation (*http://bit.ly/1oe0hIx*).

Save your changes and watch what happens. The application name updates in real time as you type into the input field! Ember's data binding at work.

See the change in this commit (*http://bit.ly/1jda66l*).

---

### When to Use .get() and .set()

If you look at enough Ember tutorials, you're bound to see someone referencing and even assigning properties on Ember objects (models, controllers, etc.) with a simple reference. For instance, if we had tried to do so in our `applicationName` computed property, it might have looked like this:

```
applicationName: function() {
  var st = this.searchTerms;
  if (st) {
    return st + "???"
  } else {
    return "Rock'n'Roll Call"
  }
}.property('searchTerms'),
```

It's generally a good idea to use the `.get()` and `.set()` methods of Ember objects, instead. These methods do more than simply reading and assigning values to properties; they are part of the `Ember.Observable` (*http://bit.ly/1oe0jQL*) mixing, and, as such, they are triggering property change events when you set the value and listening for property change events when you read the property. Using `.get()` will ensure you have the most current value of the property, even if it's been very recently changed. Using `.set()` will ensure that any other Ember objects that are observing the property you're about to change get notified when it changes.

---

## The Power of Promises and the model Method

We have a `RocknrollcallYeoman.Artist` model. We need a `RocknrollcallYeoman.Song`, too. Here it is:

```
RocknrollcallYeoman.Song = Em.Object.extend({
  id: null,
  enid: null,
  title: null,
  artist_name: null,
  artist_id: null,
  audio_md5: null,
  audio_summary: null,
  hotttnesss: null,
  track: null,
  types: null
});
```

See the change in this commit (*http://bit.ly/1jslf8x*).

---

Our `search-results` route doesn't currently have much of a model to hand off to the `SearchResultsController` we're probably going to need to build. We'll need to address that.

---

## This Is Kind of a Big Deal

There's a big lesson to be learned here: if it feels like you're writing a lot of code—too much code—to accomplish something with Ember, you're probably doing it wrong.

In this case, we made use of `setupController` (a method we haven't talked about yet) to do this next part, which is a method within your route that gets passed a fully baked controller and the model returned from your route's `model` method. Sounds like a really convenient place to write code that depends on those two pieces, right? The trick is, generally speaking, you probably don't need to and shouldn't depend on populated models and fully baked controllers. You should write loosely coupled code that leans on Ember's data binding and events. After all, that model data can change very quickly. Your controller can be extended with new properties and methods after the fact, too (see Ember.Object.reopenClass (*http://bit.ly/1qReiQc*)).

---

Our first draft of this prototype was a little spaghetti-like in this section. This next step is a little tricky. We want to take what the user typed in as a search term expression, do *two* searches against The Echo Nest's database with those terms (one search assuming the user is looking for an artist and one assuming the user is looking for a song), and then we need to operate on the results from those searches in order to create and populate some models, which we'll return to our controller.

We originally thought the best way to do this was to make use of the `setupController` method of our `SearchResultsRoute`. `setupController` is a method within your routes that is called *after* your controller is instantiated and your `model` method has returned content to the controller and you're passed a reference to each as an argument to `setupController`. From one controller object, it's pretty easy to get access to other controllers. The most obvious solution to us, on our first run through, was to create two methods in our `SearchResultsController` that each knew how to query The Echo Nest's API to create their respective models: `Artist` and `Song`.

This resulted in some confusing code. Our `SearchResultsRoute` fired its `setupController` method, which then called those two methods of the `SearchResultsController`, which made the queries against The Echo Nest, and then, with the results, created models and updated a property on the `SearchResultsController`. There's a lot of reaching around there, and it's also telling that we didn't even use the `model` method.

So we re-factored. Here's the saner version of `SearchResultsRoute`, which makes use of RSVP:

```
RocknrollcallYeoman.SearchResultsRoute = Ember.Route.extend({
  model: function (query) {
    return Promise.all([
      $.getJSON("http://developer.echonest.com/api/v4/artist/search?api_key=
      <YOUR-API-KEY>&format=json&results=10&bucket=images&bucket=hotttnesss
      &bucket=biographies&bucket=id:musicbrainz", { name: query.term }),
      $.getJSON("http://developer.echonest.com/api/v4/song/search?api_key=
      <YOUR-API-KEY>&format=json&results=10&bucket=id:7digital-US&bucket=
      audio_summary&bucket=song_hotttnesss&bucket=tracks&bucket=song_type",
      { title: query.term })
    ]).then(function(jsonArray){
      var artistResults = jsonArray[0].response.artists,
        songResults = jsonArray[1].response.songs,
        artists = [],
        songs = [],
        i = 0, entry = null;

      for (i = 0; i < artistResults.length; i++) {
        var entry = artistResults[i];
        artists.push(RocknrollcallYeoman.Artist.create({
          id: i + 1,
          type: 'artist',
          name: entry.name,
          hotttnesss: entry.hotttnesss,
          enid: entry.id
        }));
      }

      entry = null;

      for (i = 0; i < songResults.length; i++) {
        entry = songResults[i];
        songs.push(RocknrollcallYeoman.Song.create({
          id: i + 1,
          title: entry.title,
          enid: entry.id,
          type: 'song',
          artist_id: (entry.artist_id) ? entry.artist_id : null,
          artist_name: entry.artist_name,
          hotttnesss: entry.song_hotttnesss,
          audio_summary: entry.audio_summary
        }));
      }
      return {artists: artists, songs: songs}
    });

  }
});
```

Walking, briskly, through that `model` method, we return a `Promise.all` object, which only resolves and calls its `then` method when all functions passed to it have successfully resolved. We pass two functions, each of which use jQuery's `getJSON` to query The Echo Nest (once for song results and once for artist results). Our `then` method gets an array of JSON response objects, corresponding to the two queries (songs and artists), each of which are arrays of objects—the search results. We loop over each, building our own arrays of `Song` and `Artist` models. We then return an object that contains those two arrays.

So, our `model` method will return a promise which, when fulfilled, will return an object with song models and artist models corresponding to the search results appropriate for the search terms the user entered before hitting Enter or clicking the Play button.

This may still look somewhat complex. Believe us when we say it's a lot prettier than the previous version.

 You may have noticed `<YOUR-API-KEY>` in the XMLHttpRequest to the Echo Nest server:

```
$.getJSON("http://developer.echonest.com/api/v4/artist/
search? api_key=<YOUR-API-KEY>...
```

You'll need to replace this with your own API key for the Echo Nest. To do this, visit *https://developer.echonest.com/account/register* in your browser, fill out the form, and follow the directions. Once you've activated your account, find your API key on your profile page.

See the change in this commit (*http://bit.ly/1jslm40*).

Now that we have a `SearchResultsRoute`, we can move our HTML from the *app/templates/index.hbs* template to a new template. First create a new file, *app/templates/search-results.hbs*, and update it with the following:

```
<div class="search-results-wrapper clearfix">
  <div class="search-facets col-md-2">
    <h3>Show:</h3>
    <ul class="facets">
      <li>
        <label>Artists</label>
        {{view Ember.Checkbox checkedBinding="artistsIsChecked"}}
      </li>
      <li>
        <label>Songs</label>
        {{view Ember.Checkbox checkedBinding="songsIsChecked"}}
      </li>
    </ul>
  </div>
```

```
<div class="results col-md-10">
  {{#if artistsIsChecked}}
    {{#if artists.length}}
      <h3>Artists</h3>
      <ul class="search-results artists">
        {{#each artists}}
          <li>{{#link-to 'artist' enid}}{{name}} {{/link-to}}</li>
        {{/each}}
      </ul>
    {{/if}}
  {{/if}}

  {{#if songsIsChecked}}
    {{#if songs.length}}
      <h3>Songs</h3>
      <ul class="search-results songs">
        {{#each songs}}
          <li>{{#link-to 'song' enid}}"{{title}}," by {{artist_name}}
          {{/link-to}}</li>
        {{/each}}
      </ul>
    {{/if}}
  {{/if}}
</div>
</div>
```

Running through those changes, we replaced our `input` tags with `Ember.Checkbox` helpers, which will render `input` tags whose `checked` value will be bound to whatever we pass to `checkedBinding` (don't worry if you don't recognize what we passed). We added a few `#if` blocks, which conditionally show whole sections of the page based on the current value of the same thing we passed to those `Ember.Checkbox` helpers and whether the search results arrays actually have any content. If the user unchecks "songs" or if the search results array for songs is empty, we don't render that section.

Finally, we added a `link-to` to our search result `li`, linking to the routes `artist` and `song`, and passing the `enid` to each.

See the change in this commit (*http://bit.ly/1nz4OHM*).

So, we bound the checkboxes to variables called `artistsIsChecked` and `songsIsChecked`, but we havent' defined those anywhere, yet. These, dear reader, are a perfect example of the transient data that belongs in a controller—let's create a `SearchResultsController`:

```
RocknrollcallYeoman.SearchResultsController = Em.ObjectController.extend({
  artistsIsChecked: true,
  songsIsChecked: true
});
```

I hope that one didn't blow your mind.

See the change in this commit (*http://bit.ly/1kVFgSv*).

All we need now is a `SongRoute` to match our `ArtistRoute` and templates for each. Here's our SongRoute:

```
RocknrollcallYeoman.SongRoute = Ember.Route.extend({
  model: function(params) {

    //find the song byId
    var url = "http://developer.echonest.com/api/v4/song/profile?api_key=
    <YOUR-API-KEY>&format=json&bucket=audio_summary&bucket=song_hotttnesss
    &bucket=tracks&bucket=song_type&bucket=id:7digital-US",
      obj = {"id": params.enid}

    return Ember.$.getJSON(url, obj)
      //returns Promise object
        .then(function(data) {
        var entry = data.response.songs[0];
        var track = null;
        if (entry.tracks.length) track = entry.tracks[0];

        return RocknrollcallYeoman.Song.create({
          enid: entry.id,
          title: entry.title,
          hotttnesss: entry.song_hotttnesss,
          track: track,
          types: entry.song_type,
          audio_summary: entry.audio_summary,
          artist_id: entry.artist_id,
          artist_name: entry.artist_name
        });
      });
  }
});
```

See the change in this commit (*http://bit.ly/1ogB4lv*).

Now, here's our *artist.hbs* that we added back in Chapter 4:

```
<div class="entity-artist page-container">
  <div class="artist-bio-lockup clearfix">
    {{#if model.image}}
      {{#if model.license}}
        {{#if model.license.url}}
          <a {{bind-attr href="model.license.url"}}>
            <img {{bind-attr src="model.image.url"}} class="pull-right">
          </a>
        {{else}}
          <img {{bind-attr src="model.image.url"}} class="pull-right">
        {{/if}}
      {{else}}
        <img {{bind-attr src="model.image.url"}} class="pull-right">
      {{/if}}
```

```
    {{/if}}
    <h3 class="fancy">{{model.name}}</h3>
    <h4>
      {{hotttnesss-badge model.hotttnesss}}
    </h4>
    <p class="bio pull-left">Biography(from {{model.biography.site}}):
    {{model.biography.text}}</p>
    <a {{bind-attr href="model.biography.url"}} class="pull-left">Read more</a>
  </div>

  {{#if model.videos.length}}
  <div class="videos">
    <h5>Videos</h5>
    {{#each video in videos}}
      <a {{bind-attr href="video.url"}}><img {{bind-attr
      src="video.image_url"}} class="video-thumbnail"></a>
    {{/each}}
  </div>
  {{/if}}
</div>
```

And here's our new *song.hbs*:

```
<div class="entity-song page-container">
  <div class="song-lockup clearfix">
    {{#if model.track}}
      {{#if model.track.release_image}}
        <img {{bind-attr src="model.track.release_image"}} class="pull-right">
      {{/if}}
    {{/if}}
    <h3 class="fancy">{{model.title}}</h3>

    <h4>
      Artist: {{#link-to "artist" artist_id}}{{artist_name}}{{/link-to}}
    </h4>
    <h4>
      Tags:
      {{#each types}}
        <span class="badge">{{.}}</span>
      {{/each}}
    </h4>
    <h4>
      Duration: <span id="song-duration" {{bind-attr data-duration=
        "model.audio_summary.duration"}}></span>
    </h4>
    <h4>
      Tempo: {{model.audio_summary.tempo}} <abbr>BPM</abbr>
    </h4>
  </div>

</div>
```

Hopefully by now you can read those pretty easily.

---

Save your changes, and tool around. You have a web application!

See the change in this commit (*http://bit.ly/1qpFSHm*).

"But wait," you say, "we haven't even talked about views!"

# Views

You're absolutely right. Pretty interesting, no? We're six chapters and a working web application into this book, and we haven't talked about Ember's View. Think back on what we've accomplished with computed properties and data binding, though, and you'll see why. How much of your view code with other application stacks deals with updating views based on changes in data? For me, at least, I think it's safe to say almost all of it. And look at the checkbox interaction we just built. We built a simple but useful faceted, search-like interaction widget without writing any view code or declaring any events, using just data binding and the #if flow control in our template.

But there is one thing left we'd like to do that our template doesn't make very simple. The Echo Nest returns a song's duration in seconds. That's great for doing math, but it's not how humans are used to reading duration. Our *song.hbs* template is currently pushing the song duration into a data attribute because its value isn't human friendly. We can't easily convert seconds to "hh:mm:ss" with template logic, but we can use some view code.

Yes, technically, this would also be a good candidate for a computed property. Your Song model could have a computed property that does the exact same thing we're about to do. If you do this with view code, though, you could—we won't—do something interesting, like visualize the duration by spinning the hands of a clock up to the time signature, animating the numbers in flip-clock style or the like.

First, create a SongView in *app/scripts/views/song_view.js*:

```
RocknrollcallYeoman.SongView = Em.View.extend({});
```

See the change in this commit (*http://bit.ly/1hEjTTq*).

Now, let's add a didInsertElement method. didInsertElement is, to an Ember View, not unlike $().ready() is to jQuery document. It is a handler that is called once a View has been rendered and injected into the page, a safe time to assume the DOM is ready for manipulation:

```
RocknrollcallYeoman.SongView = Em.View.extend({
  didInsertElement: function() {
    $('#song-duration').text(function(){
      var $this = $(this);
      var origSeconds = $this.attr('data-duration');
      var minutes = Math.floor(origSeconds/60);
```

```
    var seconds = Math.floor(origSeconds % 60);
    return minutes + ":" + seconds
  });
  }
});
```

See the change in this commit (*http://bit.ly/1yf6ign*). Views can also respond to browser events, such as "click," like so:

```
RocknrollcallYeoman.SongView = Em.View.extend({
  click: function(jQueryEvent) {
    console.log(jQueryEvent.target);
  }
});
```

You can also specify the events you wish to respond to with a different syntax and a different approach to context, like so:

```
RocknrollcallYeoman.SongView = Em.View.extend({
  eventManager: Ember.Object.create({
    click: function(jQueryEvent, view) {
      console.log(view);
    }
  })
});
```

With this syntax, you get two arguments: the jQuery event and a View. Don't forget that you can nest Views inside one another. In our first click handler, declared right on the View, our context within our handler would always be the View (in this case, SongView). In our second version, if there was a nested View—rendered to an outlet or similar helper—and it was the target of the click event, that nested view would be given to our handler in its second argument, giving us access to both contexts.

Views get really interesting when you start looking at helpers, components, and the like, which we'll do in Chapter 9.

# Wrapping Things Up

Are you tearing up a little? I am! We just built your first Ember application! We built our own router, routes, templates, models, controllers, and views, and we learned how to keep them synchronized and working together with data binding and events. We even learned how to build a fairly complex model comprised of data from multiple queries against a third-party database! And best of all, we learned that Tom Waits' birthday is December 7!

Consider how much you've learned to do in so little code, in so little time. This is "developer ergonomics" at work.

In the remaining chapters, we will prepare our prototype for production.

CHAPTER 7

# Persisting Data

Up until this point, in Chapter 4 through Chapter 6, we have built a relatively simple prototype Ember application. We have utilized most of Ember's core functionality: router, routes, controllers, Handlebars templates, and views.

In this chapter, we are ready to begin preparing our Ember application for production. In doing so, we will explore Ember Data, the `model` class, remote persistence and RESTful web services, reusable components, and testing. There are many ways to *skin this cat,* but the approach that we prefer involves Ember App Kit.

So now you should follow along the commit history and companion code with a new repo (*https://github.com/emberjsbook/rocknrollcall-eak/commits/master*).

In this repo, you will notice that functionality introduced in Chapter 4 through Chapter 6 will be included in one single commit.

## Not Rolling Our Own Ajax

Given the high-level features that were laid out at the beginning of Chapter 4, the application persists the user's interactions as activities, building a history of the search terms. We will begin with building client-side models and persisting the data to local storage. Later, we will migrate to a solution that persists the same data to a remote, RESTful data store.

In order to understand the problems we will solve with client persistence libraries, we need to first take a look at why we would want to get away from rolling our own Ajax calls.

After all, it is possible to just use jQuery to load JSON data from a server, then use those JSON objects as *models*, performing the serialization and deserilization manually.

Here is an example of basic creation of making a request to a remote server for data, instantiating it from an Ember object, and storing it in client-side memory. We actually do this in our application with the data from the EchoNest API. Let's take a look at our songs search data.

First, we would create a basic Ember object:

```
RocknrollcallYeoman.Song = Em.Object.extend({
    id: null,
    enid: null,
    title: null,
    artist_name: null,
    artist_id: null,
    audio_md5: null,
    audio_summary: null,
    hotttnesss: null,
    track: null,
    types: null
});
```

Now, that we have the `Em.Object`, we can instantiate it and access its attributes through getters and setters:

```
var song = RocknrollcallYeoman.Song.create();
song.set('artist_name', 'Willie Nelson');
console.log(song.get('artist_name')); // Willie Nelson
```

Now, we can manually make a request for our data objects and push them to a `results` array:

```
var c = $.getJSON(
  "http://developer.echonest.com/api/v4/song/search?api_key=<YOUR-API-KEY>
  &format=json&results=10&bucket=id:7digital-US&bucket=audio_summary
  &bucket=song_hotttnesss&bucket=tracks&bucket=song_type", {
        title: term
    });

    var results = Em.A();

    c.success(function(data) {
      var entries = data.response.songs;
      for (var i = 0; i < entries.length; i++) {
        var entry = entries[i];
        results.push(RocknrollcallYeoman.Song.create({
          id: i + 1,
          title: entry.title,
          enid: entry.id,
          type: 'song',
          artist_id: (entry.artist_id) ? entry.artist_id : null,
          artist_name: entry.artist_name,
          hotttnesss: entry.song_hotttnesss,
          audio_summary: entry.audio_summary
        }));
```

```
      }
    });

        return results;
```

At this point, we know we can instantiate new objects from our model, perform *gets* and *sets* on our object instances, and make requests across the network for new data.

But, at this point we may want to abstract the network call out to a `findAll()` method so that we aren't repeating the same code over and over. In order to do this, we need to start with using `reopenClass` to define a class level method on our `Rocknroll callYeoman.Song` class. Now we can just call `RocknrollcallYeoman.Song.findAll()` to get our results:

```
RocknrollcallYeoman.Song.reopenClass({
  findAll: function(term) {
    var c = $.getJSON("http://developer.echonest.com/api/v4/song/search?
    api_key=<YOUR-API-KEY>&format=json&results=10&bucket=id:7digital-US
    &bucket=audio_summary&bucket=song_hotttnesss&bucket=tracks&
    bucket=song_type", {
      title: term
    });

    var results = Em.A();

    c.success(function(data) {
      var entries = data.response.songs;
      for (var i = 0; i < entries.length; i++) {
        var entry = entries[i];
        results.push(RocknrollcallYeoman.Song.create({
          id: i + 1,
          title: entry.title,
          enid: entry.id,
          type: 'song',
          artist_id: (entry.artist_id) ? entry.artist_id : null,
          artist_name: entry.artist_name,
          hotttnesss: entry.song_hotttnesss,
          audio_summary: entry.audio_summary
        }));
      }
    });

    return results;
  }
});
```

We could then do something similar to find a single record:

```
RocknrollcallYeoman.Song.reopenClass({
  find: function(songId) {
    var result = Ember.Object.create({});
    $.getJSON('/<echonestUrl>' + songId, function(data) {
```

```
        result.setProperties(data);
    });
    return result;
  }
});
```

And, what if we want to handle errors? Well, fortunately jQuery's `getJSON()` returns promises which helps us remove the need to manage success and error callback objects. But, as you will see later, we also can get the convenience of Promises out of libraries such as Ember Data.

And, what about setting up relationships between your models? Or handling other transport protocols like WebSocket?

The intention here is to help you understand that there is a lot to think about when you try to roll your own persistence solution and a ton of boilerplate code to write across all of your models.

# There Must Be a Better Way

Later in this chapter, we will use Ember Data to perform a similar set of tasks. As you will begin to see, our code becomes drastically simplified by using a library that manages finding the model, making changes, handling errors, and communicating across the network to the remote persistence layer using multiple protocols.

# Ember Client-Side Persistence Libraries

At the time of this writing, there are beginning to be more and more persistence solutions for Ember. Let's take a look at the available solutions.

## Ember Data

The offical, community solution. Currently, Ember Data ships as a separate library from Ember.js. It is intended to be included in core once it has matured. All of the examples provided in the companion source code use Ember Data.

## Ember Model

Ember Model (*https://github.com/ebryn/ember-model*) is a lightweight persistence solution by Eric Bryn that adds Ember primitives on top of `$.ajax`. However, it does not force you to use `$.ajax`. It provides a `model` class with some basic relationship methods, adapters, and a convenient API by using Promises.

## Ember Restless

RESTless (*http://bit.ly/1qRf7IJ*) is another lightweight persistence solution that follows a similar API to Ember Data, making it easy to understand for those familiar with Ember Data. It is considered to be full-featured enough for applications with basic CRUD requirements and supports other protocols like WebSocket.

## Ember Persistence Foundation

Another impressive solution is EPF (*https://github.com/GroupTalent/epf*). It is known to be stable and production ready. Its API is significantly different than the other solutions, following a concept of sessions to interact with the framework. It fully supports relationships and promises.

Although these solutions are worthy of further exploration, due to the limited scope of this book, our demo applicaiton, RocknRollCall, will focus on the *official* solution, Ember Data.

# An Ember Data Deep Dive

As you have most likely already gathered, Ember Data is a client-side ORM library that provides four main facilities to your Ember application:

- Loads data from a persistence layer
- Maps the data to a set of client-side models (caches them to solve for poor network latency performance)
- Updates the models
- Saves and syncs the data with a persistence layer

Ember Data is architected very modularly, designed to accomodate various protocols and data formats. This means it will work with standard RESTful JSON backends and streaming APIs like WebSocket. For real-time applications, you can open a persistent socket that pushes changes to the Ember Data store as they occur remotely. And, as you will see later, it is also easy to configure an adapter to store data locally via HTML5 local storage.

This is accomplished through abstraction layers: models, adapters, serializers, and the store. More on those to come.

## Setting Up the Router and Activity View for the Activity State

First, we need to add a new route to our router called `activity`:

```
RocknrollcallYeoman.Router.map(function() {
  this.route('activity', {
```

```
      path: 'activity'
    });
    this.resource('search-results', {
      path: 'search/:term'
    });
    this.resource('artist', {
      path: 'artist/:enid'
    });
    this.resource('song', {
      path: 'song/:sid'
    });
  });
```

See the change in this commit (*http://bit.ly/1oBANqz*).

Now, add a template named *activity.hbs* to the *app/templates/* directory and the following **each** helper to iterate over the model:

```
<h4>Total Activity Records: {{model.length}}</h4>

<ul>
  {{#each model}}
  <li class="activity">{{this.id}}</li>
  {{/each}}
</ul>
```

See the change in this commit (*http://bit.ly/1j6AHb6*).

Now, you may have noticed that this handlebars template doesn't work. You're right!
We need to give it a route handler and a model.

## Models

As you learned as early as Chapter 2 and again at the end of Chapter 5, every Ember
route has an associated model. In most cases, the model hook, or method, is used to
set up the plumbing between a particular model and a route. There are other ways,
such as an argument to {{link-to}}, or by calling a route's transitionTo() method.
In our example, we will first use the most common scenario: navigating to the activities route and fetching records from Ember Data.

```
RocknrollcallYeoman.ActivityRoute = Ember.Route.extend({
  model: function () {
    return this.store.find('activity')
  }
});
```

See the change in this commit (*http://bit.ly/1kVMDtp*).

Now that we have our route handler, we need to add a link-to helper in *app/scripts/
templates/application.hbs* to point to our new activityRoute and activity template:

```
<li>{{#link-to 'activity'}}Activity{{/link-to}}</li>
```

See the change in this commit (*http://bit.ly/1kVO4I7*). At this point, when we click our link, we should see an error in the browser console:

```
Error while loading route: Error: No model was found for 'activity'
```

That is because we also need to also build our model. So let's create a new file named *activity.js* and add it to the *app/scripts/models* directory.

Now, we can add in the necessary properties onto our model:

```
RocknrollcallYeoman.Activity = DS.Model.extend({
  display_id: DS.attr('string'),
  type: DS.attr('string'),
  display_name: DS.attr('string'),
  hotttnesss: DS.attr('number'),
  timestamp: DS.attr()
});
```

See the change in this commit (*http://bit.ly/1nszNrt*).

But wait a second. Now, we should see the error:

```
Assertion failed: Unable to find fixtures for model type RocknrollcallYeoman.
Activity
```

Well, fortunately Ember gives us an easy way to build our fixtures using JavaScript objects and attaching them to a built-in property, FIXTURES. We will get into more detail about Ember adapters, and specifically the Ember.FixtureAdapter, later in the chapter.

So, let's add these to *app/scripts/models/activity.js*:

```
RocknrollcallYeoman.Activity = DS.Model.extend({
  display_id: DS.attr('string'),
  type: DS.attr('string'),
  display_name: DS.attr('string'),
  hotttnesss: DS.attr('number'),
  timestamp: DS.attr()
});

RocknrollcallYeoman.Activity.FIXTURES = [{
  id: 0,
  display_id: "Activity1",
  type: "song",
  display_name: "On the Road Again",
  hotttnesss: 54,
  timestamp: "Fri Dec 06 2013 01:05:53 GMT-0600 (CST)"
}, {
  id: 1,
  display_id: "Activity2",
  type: "artist",
  display_name: "Willie Nelson",
  hotttnesss: 99,
```

```
        timestamp: "Fri Dec 06 2013 01:05:53 GMT-0600 (CST)"
    }];
```

See the change in this commit (*http://bit.ly/1uNxOzQ*).

 If you are interested in seeing a test-driven approach to these steps, the creation of model and tests is covered in detail in Chapter 10.

Later in this chapter, we will look at a solution for seeding Ember Data on application start. This helps development by providing content within the application, so the developer doesn't have to hardcode any dynamic content.

But for now, let's look at how the application will create data based on user interaction.

## Persisting Records Based on User Interaction

We need a way to manage user interactions and changes to our application state. Actions were covered in detail in Chapter 4, so we won't go into further detail here other than to show the specific implementation and as an example of how to create and store records with Ember Data.

As mentioned in Chapter 4, we need to declare our actions, viewedArtist and viewedSong, in the *search-results.hbs* template:

```
{{#if artistsIsChecked}}
  {{#if artists.length}}
    <h3>Artists</h3>
    <ul class="search-results artists">
      {{#each artists}}
        <li><a {{action 'viewedArtist' this }}>{{name}}</a></li>
      {{/each}}
    </ul>
  {{/if}}
{{/if}}

{{#if songsIsChecked}}
  {{#if songs.length}}
    <h3>Songs</h3>
    <ul class="search-results songs">
      {{#each songs}}
        <li><a {{action 'viewedSong' this }}>"{{title}}," by
        {{artist_name}}</a></li>
      {{/each}}
    </ul>
  {{/if}}
{{/if}}
```

See the change in this commit (*http://bit.ly/1ogJSb5*).

But, we haven't defined the actions in the `SearchResultsController`, so if we try to click and navigate to the detail view, we will receive the following error:

```
Uncaught Error: Nothing handled the action 'viewedArtist'. If you did handle
the action, this error can be caused by returning true from an action handler
in a controller, causing the action to bubble.
```

So, in the `SearchResultsController` we can define the *actions* that capture the clickable interaction, create a new Activity record, save this record, and then transition the user to the specific `ArtistRoute` or `SongRoute` by passing the ID of the object.

First, define an action:

```
actions: {
    viewedSong: function(model) {
        ...
    }
},
```

Then, create a new activity record:

```
actions: {
    viewedSong: function(model) {

        var date = Date.now();

        var activity = this.store.createRecord('activity', {
            display_id: model.enid,
            type: model.type,
            display_name: model.artist_name,
            hotttnesss: model.hotttnesss,
            timestamp: date
        });
    }
},
```

Then, save the activity record:

```
actions: {
    viewedSong: function(model) {

        var date = Date.now();

        var activity = this.store.createRecord('activity', {
            display_id: model.enid,
            type: model.type,
            display_name: model.artist_name,
            hotttnesss: model.hotttnesss,
            timestamp: date
        });

        activity.save();
```

```
        }
    },
```

See the change in this commit (*http://bit.ly/TAKP1b*).

And, finally transition the user to the new application state:

```
actions: {
    viewedSong: function(model) {

        ...

        this.transitionToRoute('song', model.enid);
    }
},
```

Here is the complete `SearchResultsController` definition of our actions:

```
actions: {

  viewedArtist: function(model) {

    var date = Date.now();

    var activity = this.store.createRecord('activity', {
      display_id: model.enid,
      type: model.type,
      display_name: model.name,
      hotttnesss: model.hotttnesss,
      timestamp: date
    });

    activity.save();

    this.transitionToRoute('artist', model.enid);
  },

  viewedSong: function(model) {

    var date = Date.now();

    var activity = this.store.createRecord('activity', {
      display_id: model.enid,
      type: model.type,
      display_name: model.artist_name,
      hotttnesss: model.hotttnesss,
      timestamp: date
    });

    activity.save();

    this.transitionToRoute('song', model.enid);
  }
},
```

See the change in this commit (*http://bit.ly/1jsuKVm*).

Although we don't show an example currently within the RocknRollCall app, there is also a `deleteRecord()` method available:

```
var activity = store.find('activity', 1);

activity.deleteRecord();

activity.save()
```

When `save` is called, Ember Data automatically formulates a XHR following standard conventions and sends an `HTTP DELETE` to the URL: `/activities/1`. Here are the `mod el.save()` and XHRs endpoints by convention:

| | | |
|---|---|---|
| Find | GET | /activities/1 |
| Find All | GET | /activities |
| Update | PUT | /activities/1 |
| Create | POST | /activities |
| Delete | DELETE | /activities/1 |

We will revisit this in Chapter 8 as we begin to build our remote persistence solution.

Finally, we can also call `destroyRecord()`, which conveniently bundles the both `dele teRecord()` and `save()` together in one call:

```
var activity = store.find('activity', 2);

activity.destroyRecord();
```

# Abstraction Layers: Store, Serializers, and Adapters

If you are paying close attention, you may have noticed that we introduced another new object without providing an explanation. Well, we did, and it was none other than the Ember Data store.

As I mentioned earlier, Ember Data provides a number of layers of abstraction; one of those abstractions is the store.

## Ember Data Store

The Ember Data store is a local cache of all the records in your application. An instance of the store (`DS.Store`) is created during application initilization and is accessible by other objects within your application, such as controllers and routes. You can interact with the store through a number of methods, such as the `find()` that was used earlier:

```
var activity = store.find('activity', 1);
```

Some other methods that are available to the Ember Data store that we have found to be quite useful are `filter()`, `all()`, and `getById()`.

### .filter()

`filter()` returns a live `RecordArray` that is bound to updates to the store:

```
store.filter('activity', function(activity){
  return activity.get('type', 'song');
});
```

### .all()

`all()` is a filter that returns all the records of a given type. It is an alternative to `find()` for uses cases when you do not want your application to make a network request to your remote persistence store:

```
store.all('activity');
```

### .getById()

Similar to `all()`, `getById()` is good for uses cases where you do not want your application to make a network request to your remote persistence store:

```
store.getById('activity',1);
```

For a complete API reference of the DS.Store, see Ember's class information page (*http://emberjs.com/api/data/classes/DS.Store.html*).

# Serializer

Another of Ember Data's abstractions is the serializer, which handles the serialization and deserialization of records as they are pushed and pulled from external data sources, such as the remote EchoNest JSON API that we communicate with in our demo application, RockNRollCall. The serializer handles the data in three distinct ways:

- Transforming attribute values
- Normalizing property names
- Serializing model's relationships

Setting up a serializer for our all of our model types is as simple as declaring it on the `ApplicationSerializer` superclass:

```
RocknrollcallYeoman.ApplicationSerializer = DS.RESTSerializer.extend({
  // ...
});
```

For more information on how to configure a Serializer to meet your needs, there is a good explanation in Ember Data's *TRANSITION.md* file (*http://bit.ly/1yfbTTS*).

### Per type serializer

Keep in mind, you can also designate a serializer on a per model type basis. So I can scope a serializer down to a specific model, without the logic impacting my other models, like so:

```
RocknrollcallYeoman.Activity = DS.Model.extend({
  // ...
});

RocknrollcallYeoman.ActivitySerializer = DS.RESTSerializer.extend({
  // ...
});
```

# Adapters

Ember Data's store can be configured to use different adapters. The FixtureAdapter and RESTAdapter are provided in core. There are other adapters written by the community, such as the LocalStorageAdapter by Ryan Florence (*https://github.com/rpflor ence*). In our RockNRollCall application, we will explore both adapters. In Chapter 8, we will take a look at setting up a backend to work with the RESTAdapter.

### FixtureAdapter

During early development and prototyping, it is beneficial to not have to stand up a server and API endpoints. The FixtureAdapter provides the ability to attach fixture data directly to your model class, which essentially stores the data in your browser's memory as JavaScript objects. The FixtureAdapter was installed by default by the Yeoman application generator, and this is what we used earlier in this chapter. Once you have built your RESTful web service backend, you can switch to the RESTAdapter without having to update your application logic.

### LocalStorageAdapter

The LocalStorageAdapter is an adapter, written by Ryan Florence, that interacts with the HTML5 `localStorage` object. HTML5 `localStorage` allows developers to store data locally within the user's browser.

First, we need to install the new dependency using Bower. We'll need to add `ember-localstorage-adapter` to *bower.json*:

```
{
  "name": "rocknrollcall-yeoman",
  "version": "0.0.0",
  "dependencies": {
```

```
    "ember": "1.3.2",
    "handlebars": "1.2.1",
    "ember-data": "1.0.0-beta.5",
    "ember-localstorage-adapter": "latest",
    "bootstrap-sass": "~3.0.0",
    "d3": "latest"
  },
  "devDependencies": {
    "ember-mocha-adapter": "0.1.2"
  }
}
```

And then, run the `install` command:

```
$ bower install
```

We also need to make sure our newly installed script is loaded into the page (it should be loaded after Ember and Ember Data):

```
<script src="bower_components/jquery/jquery.js"></script>
<script src="bower_components/handlebars/handlebars.runtime.js"></script>
<script src="@@ember"></script>
<script src="@@ember_data"></script>
<script src="bower_components/ember-localstorage-adapter/localstorage_adapter
.js"></script>
```

See the change in this commit (*http://bit.ly/1mKiNxB*).

Now, one last configuration and we should be ready to store data in our browser's LocalStorage. Open the *app/scripts/store.js* file and switch from the `FixtureAdapter` to the `LocalStorageAdapter`:

```
RocknrollcallYeoman.ApplicationAdapter = DS.LSAdapter.extend({
  namespace: 'rocknrollcall'
});
```

See the change in this commit (*http://bit.ly/1hEpjOp*).

Here, we have only one model, `Activity`; but by convention, if we use `ApplicationAdapter`, all models are run through the adapter.

We do have the capability to create multiple adapters and scope them to models. To demonstrate that, let's scope the adapter to handle only the activity data model:

```
RocknrollcallYeoman.ActivityAdapter = DS.LSAdapter.extend({
  namespace: 'rocknrollcall'
});
```

See the change in this commit (*http://bit.ly/1omhsfJ*).

### Seeding the DB with an application initializer

Application initializers are a hook point provided by Ember core that allow you to register blocks of code during your application's intialization process.

All you need to do is provide a unique name in the `name` property and implement your code within the `initialize` method. In *app/scripts/app.js*, add

```
Ember.Application.initializer({
  name: "myInitializer",

  initialize: function(container, application) {
    console.log('do something')
  }
});

var RocknrollcallYeoman = Ember.Application.create({});
```

Some common use cases for using application initializers are for registering third-party DOM `onReady` events (although keep in mind, depending on your particular use case, there may be better ways to do this provided by the framework); injecting objects like `currentUser` provided by your authentication framework into controllers, routes, and views; accessing data cached in the DOM to improve initial load performance; or seeding an Ember Data store.

In order to have something to work with for our eventual data visualization that we will build in Chapter 9, we need to create some activity records by seeding the an Ember Data Store.

So, we can implement an initializer that interacts with our LocalStorageAdapter.

We start with manually clearing `localStorage`:

```
localStorage.clear();
```

And then getting access to the store from the container:

```
store = container.lookup('store:main');
```

Then we create objects with random values:

```
for (var i = 0; i < 300; i++) {

  var id = 'ARNH6LU1187FB430FA';
  var random_id = id.split('').sort(function() {
    return 0.5 - Math.random()
  }).join('');

  var types = [
    'song',
    'artist'
  ];

  var random_type = Math.floor(Math.random() * types.length);

  var name = 'Willie Nelson';
  var random_name = name.split('').sort(function() {
    return 0.5 - Math.random()
```

```
      }).join('');

      var random_hotness = Math.floor(Math.random() * 100) + 1;
      var random_timestamp = new Date(new Date(2013, 9, 30).getTime() +
      Math.random() *
        (new Date().getTime() - new Date(2013, 9, 30).getTime()));

   };
```

And push them into the store using `createRecord()` and `save()`:

```
activity = store.createRecord('activity', {
  display_id: random_id,
  type: types[random_type],
  display_name: random_name,
  hotttnesss: random_hotness,
  timestamp: random_timestamp
});

activity.save();
```

And here is the finished product:

```
Ember.Application.initializer({
  name: "DBseeds",
  initialize: function(container, application) {

    localStorage.clear();

    store = container.lookup('store:main');
    console.log('store: ', store);

    for (var i = 0; i < 300; i++) {

      var id = 'ARNH6LU1187FB430FA';
      var random_id = id.split('').sort(function() {
        return 0.5 - Math.random()
      }).join('');

      var types = [
        'song',
        'artist'
      ];

      var random_type = Math.floor(Math.random() * types.length);

      var name = 'Jesse Cravens';
      var random_name = name.split('').sort(function() {
        return 0.5 - Math.random()
      }).join('');

      var random_hotness = Math.floor(Math.random() * 100) + 1;
       var random_timestamp = new Date(new Date(2013, 9, 30).getTime() +
```

```
        Math.random() *
          (new Date().getTime() - new Date(2013, 9, 30).getTime()));

      activity = store.createRecord('activity', {
        display_id: random_id,
        type: types[random_type],
        display_name: random_name,
        hotttnesss: random_hotness,
        timestamp: random_timestamp
      });

      activity.save();
    };

    console.log(store.find('activity')
      .then(function(stuff) {
      console.log('Total Activity Records: ' + stuff.toArray().length)
      })
    );
  }
});
```

So, each time the application is intialized, or when we refresh the page, our client-side data store will be populated with random values.

Remember the Ember Inspector from Chapter 3? Let's open up the Inspector in Google Chrome and view our records in the data store (Figure 7-1).

Nice! We should see 300 records.

See the change in this commit (*http://bit.ly/1ldDlKJ*).

# Wrapping Things Up

Now we should have a good understanding of the concepts and code necessary to set up for data persistence. In this chapter, we focused primarily on the client side with Ember Data and the LocalStorageAdapter. The Ember Data Store is configured to use the RESTAdapter by default.

In Chapter 8, we will get our backend juices flowing by taking a look at an API stub solution built into the Ember App Kit that uses Node.js and Express, along with some handy configurations to build out an API that uses the RESTAdapter.

Then, in the latter part of Chapter 8, we will build a RESTful JSON API using Rails 4 and Active Model Serializers.

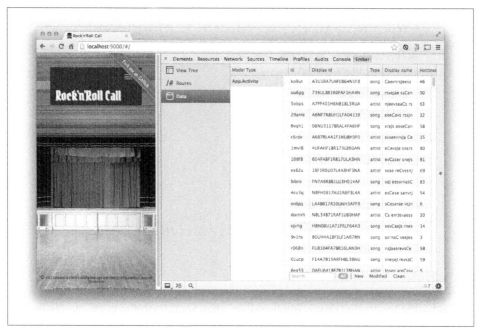

*Figure 7-1. Ember Inspector: inspecting activity records with Chrome's Inspector Extension*

In both of these examples, we switch our RocknRollCall app's adapter from the Local-StorageAdapter to the RESTAdapter. In doing so, we will experience firsthand one of the most powerful advantages to Ember Data's modularized architecture. This, along with the power of a standardized format for our JSON, enabled by Rails and Active Model Serializers, is sure to increase our development efficiency.

In other words, these features are sure to have an impact on our project workflow, as our backend development team has been building out a remote persistence solution following the same data contracts used by the frontend engineers. We can develop in parallel. And, like flipping a switch, we can now persist our data remotely or locally without changing the majority of our code.

# CHAPTER 8

# Building an Ember Backend

Ember and Ember Data are entirely client-side JavaScript, so it is possible for them to interface with any backend. In fact, that is one of the most compelling aspects of Ember Data.

There are many useful examples on the Web of developers using anything from .NET MVC (*http://www.asp.net/mvc*), Django (*https://www.djangoproject.com/*), Sinatra (*https://github.com/sinatra/sinatra*), PHP, Grails (*http://grails.org/*), and many others to deliver JSON to their Ember application. Here are a few:

- @toranb has an example RESTAdapter for Django (*http://bit.ly/1qRg5ET*).
- Microsoft provides a template for building Ember apps with .NET (*http://bit.ly/1qRg9oe*).
- The team at Travis uses Sinatra (*https://github.com/travis-ci/travis-web*).
- Ember Data is so flexible that you can also use other protocols, such as WebSocket, to push/pull data from remote data stores.
- One great example is the work by the team at Firebase (*https://www.firebase.com/*). They created a custom adapter (*https://github.com/sandersonet/ember-data-firebase*) for working with their hosted WebSocket backend.

All of this is made possible by Ember Data Adapters. By writing a custom adapter, an application can connect to any backend and any protocol accessible through a web browser.

In this chapter, we will look at building a few backends using some of today's most common web app frameworks like Express.js and Ruby on Rails. We will introduce a few new solutions to address moving our backend from local storage to a remote database. We will also address having a "server-centric" web framework to deliver our single page.

# RESTful Web Service APIs

In Chapter 7, we introduced Ember Data and the LocalStorageAdapter. Now, let's begin to explore one of the core adapters provided by default, the RESTAdapter. Here we will begin to see how our Ember application can communicate across a network with RESTful web service APIs.

---

### What Are RESTful Web Service APIs?

REST (REpresentational State Transfer), coined by Roy Fielding, refers to a stateless architecture for distributed networks. It is commonly used as a guide for a well-designed backend that exposes resources as web services, most often on the Web and over HTTP.

If you'd like to learn more about RESTful web services, be sure to check out *RESTful Web APIs* by Leonard Richardson, Mike Amundsen, and Sam Ruby (O'Reilly, 2013).

---

## Ember Data RESTAdapter

Up to this point, we have used Yeoman, which includes Yo, Grunt, and Bower, to manage our project. Our application has been completely browser based (including the persistence layer), so this solution has served us well.

Now we will introduce a new requirement to persist our data to a remote database. We also know we will want to introduce authentication in the future (out of scope for this book), so it is time to begin evaluating web-application frameworks, such as Ruby on Rails and Express.js.

We also want our Rails application to deliver our data in the JSON format and expose RESTful endpoints. In doing so, we will migrate from using the Ember Data Local-StorageAdapter to the Ember Data RESTAdapter.

## EAK (Ember App Kit) API Stubs with Express

In our companion source code, we have also provided an example using the Ember App Kit (*https://github.com/emberjsbook/rocknrollcall-eak*), mentioned in Chapter 3 and also referenced in Chapter 10.

The creators of EAK have provided a very handy Node.js/Express.js application that provides stubs to your API web service calls. This give us the ability to use the RESTadapter earlier in our project. The FixtureAdapter stores our fixtures in memory within the web browser, which is very helpful in early development and prototyping but not ideal in later development.

---

With EAK's Express API Stubs, we can configure our application to start making requests across the network to a simple web server, making our application's data calls much closer to those communicating with a real-world backend. So, let's get set up.

To get started, we need to create a new directory and clone EAK into that directory:

```
$ mkdir rocknrollcall-eak
```

```
$ cd ..
```

Next, run the following:

```
$ git clone https://github.com/stefanpenner/ember-app-kit.git
```

And now, you should have a fully functioning, starting point for an Ember application using EAK.

To install dependencies and run the application using Grunt, follow the simple Getting Started documentation available in the *README.md*.

See the change in this commit (*http://bit.ly/1oIDKpn*).

First, open the manifest file, *package.json*, and ensure APIMethod is set to stub:

```
{
  "name": "app-kit",
  "namespace": "appkit",
  "APIMethod": "stub",
  ...
```

Then, we can add an /activities route in *api-stub/routes.js*:

```
module.exports = function(server) {
  // Create an API namespace, so that the root does not
  // have to be repeated for each end point.
  server.namespace("/api", function() {

  // Return fixture data for "/api/activities"
    server.get("/activities", function(req, res) {
      var activities =
        {
          "activities": [{
            id: 0,
            display_id: "Activity1",
            searchresults_type: "song",
            display_name: "On the Road Again",
            hotttnesss: 54,
            timestamp: "Fri Dec 06 2013 01:05:53 GMT-0600 (CST)"
          }, {
            id: 1,
            display_id: "Activity2",
            searchresults_type: "artist",
            RESTful Web Service APIs | 135
            display_name: "Willie Nelson",
```

```
        hotttnesss: 99,
        timestamp: "Fri Dec 06 2013 01:05:53
        GMT-0600 (CST)"
      }]
    };
    res.send(activities);
  });
});
};
```

See the change in this commit (*http://bit.ly/1sEmBj0*).

---

# ES6 Module Syntax

If you have been following along, this is the ES6 Module syntax that was referred to in Chapter 3's references to EAK and Ember CLI. Since we are using EAK in these examples, we benefit from the ES6 Module Transpiler in our build process, which compiles down to AMD (RequireJS) syntax.

You may notice the `export default` syntax in the following code snippets. This is how it works:

EAK uses a custom resolver to resolve dependencies using naming conventions in the names of the files—for example, in the application adapter definition in the next section, it creates a file named *app/adapters/application.js* and exports the following:

```
export default DS.RESTAdapter.extend({
  namespace: 'api'
});
```

We get a module called adapters/application. Using the resolver, when Ember looks up the application adapter using this key, it will return this exported object as a module.

For more details on how the resolving dependencies works with the ES6 Module Transpiler and `export default` syntax, read more here: *https://github.com/square/ es6-module-transpiler#default-exports*.

For more details on how the resolving dependencies works in EAK, read more here: *http://iamstef.net/ember-app-kit/guides/using-modules.html*.

For more details on how the resolving dependencies works in Ember CLI, read more here: *http://iamstef.net/ember-cli/*.

---

Finally, we need to change our application adpater to extend `DS.RESTAdapter` rather than `DS.FixtureAdapter` found in *adapters/application.js*. And while we are at it, let's also add a namespace to match the Express route:

```
export default DS.RESTAdapter.extend({
  namespace: 'api'
});
```

See the change in this commit (*http://bit.ly/1jyqTWQ*).

As we have done in the beginning chapters, let's replicate some of the work we have already done. If you were following along, this should make sense to you.

Create an `Activity` model in *app/models/activity.js*:

```
var Activity = DS.Model.extend({
  display_id: DS.attr('string'),
  type: DS.attr('string'),
  display_name: DS.attr('string'),
  hotttnesss: DS.attr('number'),
  timestamp: DS.attr()
});

export default Activity;
```

See the change in this commit (*http://bit.ly/1sl5ErK*).

Now, we can update the router to include an `activities` resource:

```
var Router = Ember.Router.extend();

Router.map(function() {
  this.route('component-test');
  this.route('helper-test');
  this.resource('activities');
});

export default Router;
```

And create an `ActivityRoute` in *app/routes/activities.js*:

```
export default Ember.Route.extend({
  model: function() {
    return this.get('store').find('activity');
  }
});
```

See the change in this commit (*http://bit.ly/1g1yugM*).

To finish this off, we should add a basic activities handlebars template to iterate over the data within our HTML. Let's create:

```
<h4>Total Activity Records: {{model.length}}</h4>

<ul>
 {{#each model}}
 <li class="activity">{{this.id}}</li>
  {{/each}}
</ul>
```

See the change in this commit (*http://bit.ly/1jyrpUF*).

Now, when the `model()` hook is called when transitioning into the `/activities` route, the store is "smart" enough to use the RESTAdapter, as shown in Figure 8-1.

*Figure 8-1. Activity data and the RESTAdapter*

As mentioned in the Preface and alluded to throughout this text, as pro developers, we should be very interested in optimizing our workflow and finding efficiencies in our development process. Failing to point out aspects of Ember's modularity and their impact on real-world projects, would be missing some of the most impressive aspects of Ember and Ember Data.

That being said, there are three important concepts to take notice of here: first, switching the adapter was as simple as extending from a different class; and perhaps even more importantly, the rest of our code did not change. Second, we have provided a fully functioning specification to our backend developers. In rapid-application-development world, this is far more valuable than a documented API or a formal data diagram. Finally, our backend developers are working in parallel, and once they have an API server set up, we can switch our Ember application to point to it instead by opening our manifest file, *package.json*, and setting APIMethod to *proxy*:

```
{
  "name": "app-kit",
  "namespace": "appkit",
```

```
      "APIMethod": "proxy",
  ...
```

Then, we need to provide a URL to pass all the API calls to:

```
{
  "name": "app-kit",
  "namespace": "appkit",
  "APIMethod": "proxy",
  "proxyURL": "http://whatever.api:3232",
  ...
```

Well, there is a lot of "goodness" here. Now let's take a look at what another popular web framework, Ruby on Rails, can offer us as an alternative.

# Why Use Rails?

Let me first start off with the statement that there is no magical bullet in web application development. Framework choice is often based upon the experience of the development team and its appetite to risk trying something new versus reaping the efficiencies of coding in a framework in which it's already familiar.

That being said, if Ruby or Rails are your things, there are a number of features that can make Ember and Ember data backend development easier:

- Rails helps you manage your Ruby code, server-side MVC.
- Active Record provides an ORM for interacting with your data.
- Rails Asset Pipeline and the `ember-rails` gem help you manage your assets.
- Active Model Serializers provide the REST API that the Ember Data RESTAdapter expects by default.
- Testing is built-in.

Let's take a closer look. In this section, we will accomplish two main goals:

- Use Rails MVC to deliver a *single page* that contains our necessary Ember dependencies
- Develop simple RESTful Web Services for our `Activity` model that can communicate with Ember Data.

## Managing Dependencies with RVM (Ruby Version Manager) and Bundler

To keep our application's dependencies in order, we need to use a couple of tools. This is a simple process that can save you hours in the long run.

To begin, we will need to install RVM (Ruby Version Manager). Fortunately, the RVM documentation is fantastic and available here: *http://rvm.io/rvm/install*.

Then, install and use Ruby 2.0:

```
$ rvm install 2.0.0-p353
$ rvm use 2.0.0-p353
```

Next, we create a gemset (think of a gemset as an isolated set of your Ruby dependencies):

```
$ rvm gemset create rocknrollcall-rails
```

and run the following:

```
$ rvm --ruby-version use 2.0.0-p353@rocknrollcall-rails
```

This generates two files:

- *.ruby-version*
- *.ruby-gemset*

These files automatically set your environment to these when you migrate to the root of the application directory. These configurations can be versioned; so when a new developer clones your repository, her RVM automatically reads from these properties.

Now, to double-check ourselves, let's confirm that we are using the correct gemset. The following command should return the name that we just created (in our case, `rocknrollcall-rails`):

```
$ rvm gemset name

rocknrollcall-rails
```

Now we can install Bundler and run bundle:

```
$ gem install bundler
```

## Installing Rails

It's time now to install Ruby on Rails:

```
$ gem install rails
```

and verify the install:

```
$ rails -v
```

## Generating the Initial Application

Let's generate a basic Ruby on Rails application:

```
$ rails new rocknrollcall-rails
```

This should create the following directory structure:

```
$ ls

app/
bin/
config/
db/
lib/
log/
public/
test/
tmp/
vendor/
config.ru
Gemfile
Gemfile.lock
Rakefile
README.rdoc
```

Now you can start your application server:

```
$ cd rocknrollcall-rails

$ rails server
```

and visit localhost:3000. You should see your basic Rails application, as shown in Figure 8-2.

See the change in this commit (*http://bit.ly/1iJMbQo*).

## Updating the Gemfile

If you open the current Gemfile, you will see that by default, you have quite a few gems being loaded. The following is all you will need, so you can remove the others:

```
source 'https://rubygems.org'
ruby '2.0.0'

# Bundle edge Rails instead: gem 'rails', github: 'rails/rails'
gem 'rails', '4.1.1'

# Use sqlite3 as the database for Active Record
gem 'sqlite3'

# Use Uglifier as compressor for JavaScript assets
gem 'uglifier', '>= 1.3.0'

# Use jquery as the JavaScript library
gem 'jquery-rails'
```

*Figure 8-2. Basic Rails application*

Now run `bundle` to install the right gems:

```
$ bundle update
```

See the change in this commit (*http://bit.ly/1sl6RiP*).

## Removing TurboLinks

Be sure this was removed from our Gemfile in the previous section:

```
gem 'turbolinks'
```

TurboLinks is JavaScript that is included by default in Rails applications. TurboLinks scans your HTML on page load for links and sets up an event listener that intercepts the default action of each click event. The "page" is then fetched via `XMLHttpRequest`, replacing only the body of the page with the response. Then, it uses `PushState` to change to mimic a traditional URL.

This functionality is very redundant to the way in which the Ember router manages the state of your application. Therefore, we need to remove this functionality altogether.

Remove the following from *application.js*:

```
//= require turbolinks
```

And finally, remove "data-turbolinks-track" ⇒ true from *application.html.erb*:

```
<!DOCTYPE html>
<html>
<head>
  <title>Rocknrollcall-Rails</title>
  <%= stylesheet_link_tag "application", media: "all" %>
  <%= javascript_include_tag "application" %>
  <%= csrf_meta_tags %>
</head>
<body>

<%= yield %>

</body>
</html>
```

See the change in this commit (*http://bit.ly/1jawAuJ*).

## Understanding Rails MVC and the Single-Page Application

For the purposes of this type of application, we'll replace the contents of the default *index.html* file with our Ember app.

We won't attempt to recreate the Rails Guides (*http://edgeguides.rubyonrails.org/ 4_0_release_notes.html*) available from the Ruby on Rails community, so for a complete understanding of Ruby on Rails, the guides are great place to start.

For our needs, we will be using a very light implementation of Rails. Most of our application will exist in JavaScript, and the Rails server will provide our RESTful web services.

First, migrate to our new application directory:

```
$ cd rocknrollcall-rails
```

We can remove the default page, if it exists:

```
$ rm public/index.html
```

**Removing public/index.html**

In later versions of Rails, it is no longer necessary to remove *public/ index.html* manually. The welcome page is now managed within the Rails gem: *.rbenv/versions/2.0.0-p353/lib/ruby/gems/2.0.0/gems/ railties-4.0.0/lib/rails/templates/rails/welcome/index.html.erb*.

Now, it's time to generate our first Rails controller. Rails controllers are very different than Ember controllers. In Rails, the controller receives the request, interacts with a model to read or write data, and syncs that data with a view to create HTML output.

As described in Chapter 6, Ember controllers are different, as they exist primarily to store transient data (whether standalone or made up of data retrieved from models) or to *decorate your models with display logic.*

We will use Rails built-in generators to create one action, *index*, on our home controller. It is here, and also in the views, that you will begin to see the most difference between our modern, single-page web application and a traditional web application.

In a traditional architecture application, each controller would contain numerous actions returning an HTML page, most with web forms, for each action to be performed on the controller.

In the case of our modern web application, we will only need a single page. This is where the term *single-page application* comes from. Single-page application architecture actually employs dual MVC architecture, in that you have models, views, and controllers written in both the server-side language (in this case, Ruby) and also in JavaScript. As you will see, our MVC implementation will be *light* on the server, and most of our complexity will be managed in the client-side MVC:

```
$ rails generate controller home index

      create    app/controllers/home_controller.rb
       route    get "home/index"
      invoke    erb
      create    app/views/home
      create    app/views/home/index.html.erb
      invoke    test_unit
      create    test/controllers/home_controller_test.rb
      invoke    helper
      create    app/helpers/home_helper.rb
      invoke    test_unit
      create    test/helpers/home_helper_test.rb
```

The HomeController should now have an index action:

```
class HomeController < ApplicationController
  def index
  end
end
```

By convention, there is also an *index.html.erb* file located in *views/home/*:

```
<h1>Home#index</h1>
<p>Find me in app/views/home/index.html.erb</p>
```

See the change in this commit (*http://bit.ly/1l3zv5g*).

Now update your *routes.rb* file by setting the root to point to the index action on the StaticController:

```
Rocknrollcall::Application.routes.draw do
  get "home/index"
```

```
    root :to => 'home#index'
  end
```

The index view for the application should now look like Figure 8-3.

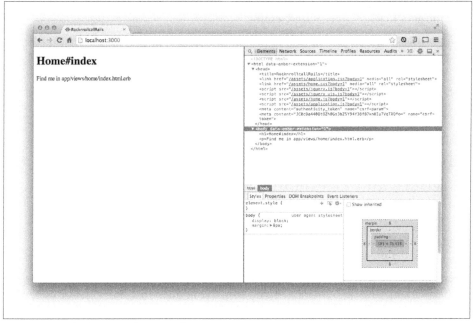

*Figure 8-3. The home index view for our SPA*

See the change in this commit (*http://bit.ly/QAzRH4*).

## Running Tests

For now, it is not important that you understand completely how Rails helps with managing tests. Ember testing will be discussed in more detail in Chapter 10.

What is important is that you get in the practice of running your test suites prior to committing your code. So, let's do just that.

But first, you need to run the rake db migrations task to create your test database:

```
$ rake db:migrate
```

Then, run your tests:

```
$ rake test
Run options: --seed 15945

# Running tests:

Finished tests in 0.049580s, 20.1694 tests/s, 20.1694 assertions/s.
```

```
1 tests, 1 assertions, 0 failures, 0 errors, 0 skips
```

## Adding Ember

Add the gem to your application Gemfile:

```
gem 'ember-rails'
gem 'ember-source', '1.0.0.rc6' # or the version you need
gem 'handlebars-source', '1.0.0.rc4' # or the version you need
```

Install the dependencies:

```
$ bundle install
```

See the change in this commit (*http://bit.ly/STC9TP*).

You should see a few new gems installed:

```
Installing active_model_serializers 0.8.1
Installing handlebars-source 1.0.0.rc4
Installing ember-source 1.0.0.rc6
Installing barber 0.4.2
Installing ember-data-source 0.14
Installing ember-rails 0.14.1
```

Then, in your environment files (i.e., *development.rb, production.rb*), configure the Ember variant (this is optional—if you don't configure this, the version of Ember used defaults to development when the Rails environment is in development, and similarly for production):

```
config.ember.variant = :development # or :production
```

Finally, generate the Ember.js application structure. Ember.js apps are not required to follow an organized file structure. The follwing generator will create the necessary stubbed dependencies in *app/assets/javascripts*:

```
$ rails generate ember:bootstrap
      insert  app/assets/javascripts/application.js
      create  app/assets/javascripts/models
      create  app/assets/javascripts/models/.gitkeep
      create  app/assets/javascripts/controllers
      create  app/assets/javascripts/controllers/.gitkeep
      create  app/assets/javascripts/views
      create  app/assets/javascripts/views/.gitkeep
      create  app/assets/javascripts/routes
      create  app/assets/javascripts/routes/.gitkeep
      create  app/assets/javascripts/helpers
      create  app/assets/javascripts/helpers/.gitkeep
      create  app/assets/javascripts/components
      create  app/assets/javascripts/components/.gitkeep
      create  app/assets/javascripts/templates
      create  app/assets/javascripts/templates/.gitkeep
```

```
create  app/assets/javascripts/templates/components
create  app/assets/javascripts/templates/components/.gitkeep
create  app/assets/javascripts/mixins
create  app/assets/javascripts/mixins/.gitkeep
create  app/assets/javascripts/rocknrollcall_rails.js
create  app/assets/javascripts/router.js
create  app/assets/javascripts/store.js
```

The generator will also add the necessary bootstrapping to *app/assets/javascripts/application.js*. By default, it uses the Rails application's name and creates a *rails_app_name.js* file to set up application namespace and initial requires:

```
//= require handlebars
//= require ember
//= require ember-data
//= require_self
//= require rocknrollcall-rails
RocknRollCallRails = Ember.Application.create();
```

Now, you should see the necessary dependencies included in your web application, like Figure 8-4.

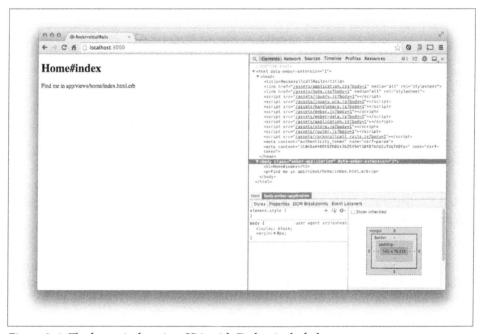

*Figure 8-4. The home index view SPA with Ember included*

Later, if you want to update to the latest builds of Ember and Ember Data, first kill your server. On both Windows and Mac OS X, press Ctrl+C. Then, run:

```
$ rails generate ember:install --head
```

Now, be sure to run the available tests:

```
$ rake test
Run options: --seed 22801

# Running tests:

Finished tests in 0.144108s, 6.9392 tests/s, 6.9392 assertions/s.

1 tests, 1 assertions, 0 failures, 0 errors, 0 skips
```

And finally, don't forget to restart your server.

See the change in this commit (*http://bit.ly/1lcs22S*).

### jquery-rails Versions

At the time of this writing, you will receive the following error if you use the latest `jquery-rails` gem:

```
Assertion failed: Ember Views require jQuery 1.7, 1.8,
1.9, 1.10, or 2.0

gem "active_model_serializers"
```

To fix this, add in an earlier version of `jquery-rails` gem that uses jQuery 1.10:

```
# Use jquery as the JavaScript library
gem 'jquery-rails', "3.0.3"

$ bundle update
```

See the change in this commit (*http://bit.ly/1iJQJGw*).

## Active Model Serializers

You may have noticed in your console output earlier, after running bundle update with the `ember-rails` gem, that the `active_model_serializers` gem was installed as a dependency:

```
Installing active_model_serializers 0.8.1
```

ActiveModel::Serializers make the formatting of our JSON API easier by helping us build JSON APIs through serializer objects. They not only provide some syntactical improvements but also a dedicated place to fully customize the JSON output.

More to come once we have a model, route, and controller set up.

## Generating the Activity model and controller

First, we need to generate a new controller with an index action (later in our application development, it will be necessary to add the remaining actions necessary to create, update, and delete Activities, but for now we will only need to provide *read-only* services to Ember Data):

```
$ rails g controller Activities index
```

which generates the following file:

```
class ActivitiesController < ApplicationController
  def index
  end
end
```

And we can update it with a simple `render` command that requests JSON as the format and all of the `Activity` models records in the database:

```
class ActivitiesController < ApplicationController
  def index
    render json: Activity.all
  end
end
```

See the change in this commit (*http://bit.ly/1hHue16*).

And, also generate the `Activity` model, by using the built-in scaffolding provided by Rails. In the following command, we can generate an `Activity` model and pass attributes along with their datatype. Rails will automatically add these attributes to the activities table in the database and map it back to the `Activity` model:

```
$ rails g model Activity display_id:string searchresults_type:string display_name:string
    timestamp:datetime hotttnesss:decimal
```

See the change in this commit (*http://bit.ly/1qwjFHG*).

Now we need to run our database migrations. Database migrations provide an easy and consistent way to version your database schema over time.

Fortunately, the generate model command also created this migration for us—all we have to do is execute it!

```
class CreateActivities < ActiveRecord::Migration
  def change
    create_table :activities do |t|
      t.string :display_id
      t.string :searchresults_type
      t.string :display_name
      t.datetime :timestamp
      t.integer :hotttnesss
      t.timestamps
    end
  end
end
```

To execute it, we again use a `rake` task:

```
$ rake db:migrate
```

Finally, we have new tests that were generated for us. So, let's run them and commit our changes:

```
$ rake test
Run options: --seed 21992

# Running tests:

........

Finished tests in 0.254310s, 31.4577 tests/s, 55.0509 assertions/s.

2 tests, 2 assertions, 0 failures, 0 errors, 0 skips
```

### Generating and configuring our serializers

As mentioned earlier, now that we have an Actvity model and a Controller, we have enough to return JSON data our Ember client.

One thing you may have noticed is that `type` is a reserved word and really shouldn't be used as a property on a model. Let's change this to `searchresults_type` because this is actually an opportunity to demonstrate the kind of serializations you can do with our activity serializer.

Here, we need to make the key in the outputted JSON be different from its name in `ActiveRecord`, `searchresults_type`. To do so, we declare the attribute with a different name and redefine that method. Now, our Ember application can remain as is, utilizing the `type` attribute on the frontend.

First, let's generate a serializer:

```
$ rails g serializer activity
```

See the change in this commit (*http://bit.ly/1mhNVBJ*).

Then, configure it:

```
class ActivitySerializer < ActiveModel::Serializer

  # look up searchresults_type on the model, but use type in the JSON
  def type
    object.searchresults_type
  end

  attributes :id, :display_id, :type, :display_name, :hotttnesss, :timestamp
end
```

See the change in this commit (*http://bit.ly/1nFgfxD*).

## Updating the router

Now, we can tell our router that we have a resource available at the URL */activities*. Like a lot of tasks, this is really simple in Ruby on Rails. Just open up *config/routes.rb* and change the declaration to call the index method on the activities controller:

```
get "activities/index"
```

to a resource declaration:

```
resources :activities
```

See the change in this commit (*http://bit.ly/1om8hvP*).

## Seeding data

Rails provides a simple way to seed our database with a few `Activity` objects. First, create some objects within *db/seeds.rb*:

```
Activity.create(
  :display_id => 'Activity1',
  :searchresults_type => 'song',
  :display_name => "On the Road Again",
  :timestamp => "Fri Dec 06 2013 01:05:53 GMT-0600 (CST)",
  :hotttnesss => 54
)

Activity.create(
  :display_id => 'Activity2',
  :searchresults_type => 'artist',
  :display_name => "Willie Nelson",
  :timestamp => "Fri Dec 06 2013 01:05:53 GMT-0600 (CST)",
  :hotttnesss => 99
)
```

And be sure to run the task to push the data into the database:

```
$ rake db:seed
```

Now, you should be able to start your server and access the data through a web service call to *http://localhost:3000/activities*:

```
$ rails server
```

See the change in this commit (*http://bit.ly/1jyz71g*).

The results should look something like Figure 8-5.

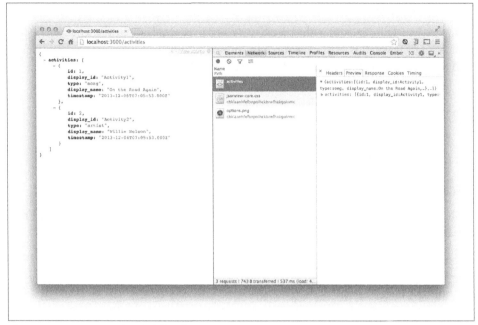

*Figure 8-5. Activities RESTful web service*

# Wrapping Things Up

In this chapter, we used two different web app frameworks to move our backend from local storage to a remote database using the Ember Data RESTAdapter and RESTful web service endpoints. By using Ember App Kit's built-in Node.js/Express.js implementation, we were able to migrate to the RESTAdapter through configuration changes.

We also showed how to configure Ruby on Rails to deliver a single page and added active model serializers to format our JSON output.

# CHAPTER 9
# Ember Components

No matter what environment you find yourself working in, creating componentization and reuse of functionality is a common goal for development teams. Historically, achieving reuse has been difficult. First of all, building a piece of code generic enough to meet unknown requirements is rarely a complete success and takes years of experience, not to mention a wide view of the goals (past and future) of the product you are building. Also, until recently, there has not been a standard. So the technical options have been to make use of UI toolkits, iframes, or proprietary widget/gadget specifications.

The Web Components specification breathes new life into this challenge area by providing numerous related "subspecifications" (Custom Elements, Shadow DOM, HTML Imports) that can be used together to create standardized encapsulation of UI widgets.

Ember components follow the Web Components specifications closely, providing the essentials, or polyfilling, the necessary functionality in less capable browsers. The idea is that as browsers continue to adopt these specifications, Ember is smart enough to use the native functionality when it is available. So, developers can begin to write Web Components now, as "future-friendly" Ember components.

In this chapter, we will first build a simple component to demonstrate the basics. Then we will move into a more complex component that integrates a third-party library (in this case, D3.js) into the Ember application. To do so, we will continue working with our Yeoman managed application (*http://bit.ly/1qRaRcr*).

First, let's take care of a bit of housekeeping. We are going to need to create a directory to include our components. So, let's add *app/scripts/components*.

Then, we will need to add a `require` call to *app/scripts/app.js* to make sure Grunt's build task picks up the new file and includes it in *app/scripts/combined-scripts.js*:

```
/* Order and include as you please. */
require('scripts/controllers/*');
require('scripts/components/*');
require('scripts/store');
require('scripts/models/*');
require('scripts/routes/*');
require('scripts/views/*');
require('scripts/router');
```

See the change in this commit (*http://bit.ly/1iKoyHC*).

 If you are using a later version of the Yeoman Ember generator, this
may have already been done for you.

# The Anatomy of an Ember Component

There are a few pieces to the component puzzle, but overall component creation is a
really straightforward process. In this section, we will walk through the steps of turn-
ing an `Activity` content into a reusable component.

## Create a Template

The first step is to decide on a name for your component, create the *app/scripts/
components* directory, and add a new file named *activity_log_component.js*:

```
RocknrollcallYeoman.ActivityLogComponent = Ember.Component.extend({});
```

It is necessary to include a dash in the name per the proposed specification. This is
intended to help prevent clashes with other native elements.

For our simple example, we can use this in *templates/activity.hbs*:

```
{{activity-log}}
```

In our example applications, we are using build tools, so we can create a new directory at *templates/components*, and populate it with a new Handlebars template named
*activity-log.hbs*:

```
I am an Activity Log.
<hr>
```

In *activity.hbs*, we can loop through this template, based on the current model provided by the ActivityRoute's `model()` hook:

```
{{#each}}
  {{activity-log}}
{{/each}}
```

The log should now look like Figure 9-1.

*Figure 9-1. ActivityLog Ember component: simple text*

See the change in this commit (*http://bit.ly/1gvTEyz*).

And, make the *activity-log.hbs* a little more complex by adding in the model's properties:

```
<p> display_id: {{display_id}}</p>
<p> type: {{type}}</p>
<p> display_name: {{display_name}}</p>
<p> hotttnesss: {{hotttnesss}}</p>
<p> timestamp: {{timestamp}}</p>

<hr>
```

See the change in this commit (*http://bit.ly/1nPGWA0*).

In order to pull this off, we have to update the Handlebars as well by passing each property from the current template's scope to the component.

We can change the property names here or just keep the same. For simplicity, we will just keep them all the same. In *activity.hbs*, add the following:

```
{{#each}}
  {{activity-log display_id=display_id type=type display_name=display_name
      hotttnesss=hotttnesss timestamp=timestamp }}
{{/each}}
```

See the change in this commit (*http://bit.ly/1jT3nTY*).

Now we should see the properties rendered, as in Figure 9-2.

*Figure 9-2. ActivityLog Ember component: model properties*

## Extending Ember.Component

Now, if we just wanted to wrap up static HTML into reusable, or even pass minimal properties through to our component's scope, we can manage our Ember component all within our templates.

But, if we need to do a little more, such as changing the wrapping element, integrating with a third-party JavaScript library such as jQuery or D3, or handle *actions* similar to those presented earlier in this book, then we need to make use of extending the Ember.Component class.

Fortunately, naming conventions allow us to create a new subclass by removing the hyphen, camel-casing the class name, and adding Component on the end. Ember automagically knows which component it is referencing. For example, our previous example activity log would be subclassed as so:

```
RocknrollcallYeoman.ActivityLogComponent = Ember.Component.extend({});
```

# Building a Heat Map Visualization with D3

Now that we know how to subclass, let's take the same data we used for the `Activity LogComponent` and create a custom heat-map animation using the D3.js visualization library. D3.js is a JavaScript library for manipulating HTML, SVG, and CSS based on data. For more on D3.js, check out the documentation (*http://d3js.org/*).

First, we need to get the D3 library onto our page. So, we will make an update to our *bower.json* file, adding the latest from D3:

```
{
  "name": "rocknrollcall-yeoman",
  "version": "0.0.0",
  "dependencies": {
    "ember": "1.3.2",
    "handlebars": "1.2.1",
    "ember-data": "1.0.0-beta.5",
    "ember-localstorage-adapter": "latest",
    "bootstrap-sass": "~3.0.0",
    "d3": "latest"
  },
```

See the change in this commit (*http://bit.ly/1geYPrT*).

Now, run:

```
$ bower install
```

And, finally add a `script` tag to the *app/index.html* file:

```
<script src="bower_components/d3/d3.js"></script>
```

See the change in this commit (*http://bit.ly/1geZOUf*).

Now, we are interested in using the hotttnesss property and the timestamp property to build a heat-map grid that includes "Days of the Week" on the y-axis, and "Times of the Day" on the x-axis. Each square in the grid reprensents an hour of a specific day. The color of the square depicts the hotttnesss of your last search within the hour, dark being lower on the hotttnesss scale and lighter being higher on the scale. A color legend is also included to aid the viewer.

We are not going to discuss the internals of D3 here, as it is out of scope for this book. The intention of this example is to show how to integrate a third-party library like D3 into your component.

So let's get started with the basic structure of our `Component` subclass. The top of our class declaration will be used to manage specific properties that we can reference from within the two methods: `draw()` and `didInsertElement()`.

`didInsertElement()` is called when the outer element of the component has been inserted into the DOM. So we can override this function to do any set up that requires accessing an element in the document body. Here, we will get the data from the controller and pass it to draw.

draw() contains the majority of the D3-specific logic. If you're following along, you'll begin to see that this pattern could be used for many different types of visualizations that take data as an input and pass that data to render() or draw() logic:

```
RocknrollcallYeoman.HeatMapComponent = Ember.Component.extend({

    width: 900,
    height: 280,

    draw: function(myData){
      // draw the heat map
    },

    didInsertElement: function(){
      var data = this.get('controller.data.content');
      this.draw(data);
    }
});
```

Before we pass the data to draw(), we can "prep" it a bit to translate it into an array. This is a common thing to do, and didInsertElement() is an acceptable place to perform this logic:

```
RocknrollcallYeoman.HeatMapComponent = Ember.Component.extend({

    width: 900,
    height: 280,

    draw: function(myData){
      // draw the heat map
    },

    didInsertElement: function(){
      var data = this.get('controller.data.content');
      var hotnessArray = [];
      for (var i=0;i<data.length;i++) {
        var date = new Date(data[i].get('timestamp'));
        var row = {};
        row.day = date.getDay() + 1;
        row.hour = date.getHours() + 1;
        row.value = data[i].get('hotttnesss');
        hotnessArray.push(row);
      }
      this.draw(hotnessArray);
    }
});
```

So, as we did in our simple ActivityLogComponent, we can create a Handlebars template at *templates/components/heat-map.hbs*.

Within this template, all we will need is a `div` element with an `id`:

```
<div id="chart"></div>
```

Now we can add the helper to *templates/activity.hbs*:

```
{{heat-map data=model}}
```

Here is the finished `HeatMapComponent`. As you can see, our D3 logic is encapsulated nicely inside of the `draw()` method. Now, add this to *app/scripts/components/heat_map_component.js*:

```
RocknrollcallYeoman.HeatMapComponent = Ember.Component.extend({
  margin: { top: 50, right: 0, bottom: 100, left: 30 },
  width: 900,
  height: 280,
  gridSize: 37,
  legendElementWidth: 100,
  buckets: 9,
  colors: ["#2F0000","#661201","#911900","#B22604","#CB3804","#F25B02",
  "#F2720D","#FFA321","#FAC40A"], // alternatively colorbrewer.YlGnBu[9]
  days: ["Mo", "Tu", "We", "Th", "Fr", "Sa", "Su"],
  times: ["1a", "2a", "3a", "4a", "5a", "6a", "7a", "8a", "9a", "10a", "11a",
"12a", "1p",
    "2p", "3p", "4p", "5p", "6p", "7p", "8p", "9p", "10p", "11p", "12p"],

  draw: function(myData){
    var self = this;
    this.set('data',myData);
    var svg = d3.select('#'+self.get('elementId'));
    var colorScale = d3.scale.quantile()
      .domain([10, 100])
      .range(self.colors);

    var svg = d3.select("#chart").append("svg")
      .attr("width", self.width + self.margin.left + self.margin.right)
      .attr("height", self.height + self.margin.top + self.margin.bottom)
      .append("g")
        .attr("transform", "translate(" + self.margin.left + "," + self.mar
gin.top + ")");

    var dayLabels = svg.selectAll(".dayLabel")
      .data(self.days)
      .enter().append("text")
      .text(function (d) { return d; })
      .attr("x", 0)
      .attr("y", function (d, i) { return i * self.gridSize; })
      .style("text-anchor", "end")
      .attr("transform", "translate(-6," + self.gridSize / 1.5 + ")")
      .attr("class", function (d, i) { return ((i >= 0 && i <= 4) ?
        "dayLabel mono axis axis-workweek" : "dayLabel mono axis"); });

    var timeLabels = svg.selectAll(".timeLabel")
```

```
      .data(self.times)
      .enter().append("text")
      .text(function(d) { return d; })
      .attr("x", function(d, i) { return i * self.gridSize; })
      .attr("y", 0)
      .style("text-anchor", "middle")
      .attr("transform", "translate(" + self.gridSize / 2 + ", -6)")
      .attr("class", function(d, i) { return ((i >= 7 && i <= 16) ?
        "timeLabel mono axis axis-worktime" : "timeLabel mono axis"); });

  var heatMap = svg.selectAll(".hour")
    .data(self.data)
    .enter().append("rect")
    .attr("x", function(d) { return (d.hour - 1) * self.gridSize; })
    .attr("y", function(d) { return (d.day - 1) * self.gridSize; })
    .attr("rx", 4)
    .attr("ry", 4)
    .attr("class", "hour bordered")
    .attr("width", self.gridSize)
    .attr("height", self.gridSize)
    .style("fill", self.colors[0]);

  heatMap.transition().duration(1000)
    .style("fill", function(d) { return colorScale(d.value); });

  heatMap.append("title").text(function(d) { return d.value; });

  var legend = svg.selectAll(".legend")
    .data([0].concat(colorScale.quantiles()), function(d) { return d; })
    .enter().append("g")
    .attr("class", "legend");

  legend.append("rect")
    .attr("x", function(d, i) { return self.legendElementWidth * i; })
    .attr("y", self.height)
    .attr("width", self.legendElementWidth)
    .attr("height", self.gridSize / 2)
    .style("fill", function(d, i) { return self.colors[i]; });

  legend.append("text")
    .attr("class", "mono")
    .text(function(d) { return "≥ " + Math.round(d*10)/10; })
    .attr("x", function(d, i) { return self.legendElementWidth * i; })
    .attr("y", self.height + self.gridSize);
},

didInsertElement: function(){
  var data = this.get('controller.data.content');
  var hotnessArray = [];
  for (var i=0;i<data.length;i++) {
    var date = new Date(data[i].get('timestamp'));
    var row = {};
```

```
        row.day = date.getDay() + 1;
        row.hour = date.getHours() + 1;
        row.value = data[i].get('hotttnesss');
        hotnessArray.push(row);
      }
      this.draw(hotnessArray);
    }
  });
```

See the change in this commit (*http://bit.ly/1uV4RC9*).

And now our `HeatMapComponent` shows the `Activity` model data we created in Chapter 8, as shown in Figure 9-3.

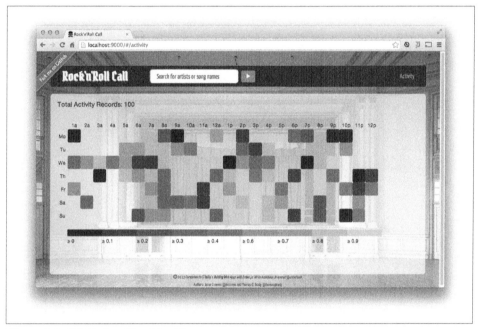

*Figure 9-3. D3 Ember HeatMapComponent*

# Wrapping Things Up

As you can see, by following web standards, the Ember team has given us an elegant way to write reusable, encapsualted widgets that can make our applications more maitainable and easier to extend moving forward. If you have tried to write maintainable, production code, you know this is typically a high priority for most technical teams and rarely easy to do.

In the next and final chapter, we will address another important concept for production-ready applications: testing.

# CHAPTER 10

# Ember Testing

If you've kept up with the Ember testing over the last year, there has been quite a bit of debate within the Ember community about testing best practices. Well, what would you expect? That's just how testing goes.

When putting together the testing strategy for this book, we wanted to base on it on our experience with real-world application development. In doing so, one of our guiding principles is to keep our strategy as simple as possible, without sacrificing test coverage.

We also wanted readable tests, because they act as the development team's primary source of "enforced" and tested requirements. It is also important to us that our test runner be fast to ensure we are not impeding developer productivity, and we'd like the test runner to integrate with a CI server easily. Finally, it's important to obtain test coverage over as much code that makes sense for our particular application.

We will explore a basic integration and unit-testing approach with a simple setup provided by Ember App Kit. This setup uses Qunit, Ember testing helpers, and the Testem test runner.

One thing that is certain is that there are as many testing strategies as there are development teams, so hopefully the following examples give you enough exposure to the basics for you to start formulating your own strategy to fit your application, team, and development timeline.

The Ember Guides provide a great reference for setting up a basic testing scenario, so we won't be redundant in rehashing that documentaiton. We will assume you have read the Ember Guides page on Integration Testing (*http://emberjs.com/guides/test ing/integration/*) to have full context of the following information.

# Ember Testing with Ember App Kit, Qunit, and Testem

The source code for this initial example is included here: *https://github.com/emberjs-book/rocknrollcall-eak*.

rocknrollcall-eak (*https://github.com/emberjsbook/rocknrollcall-eak*) uses QUnit, Ember Testing, and Testum Test Runner.

If you have been following along in this book, you will have seen that there is an `Ac tivity` model that *records* data associated to the user's searches. For our basic unit testing example, let's use this model and the associated route and template.

To start, let's set up our first test. Fortunately, Ember App Kit has handled our boiler-plate within a couple of files starting with *test_helper.js*:

```
document.write('<div id="ember-testing-container"><div id="ember-testing">
</div></div>');

Ember.testing = true;

window.startApp          = require('appkit/tests/helpers/start_app')['default'];
window.isolatedContainer  =  require('appkit/tests/helpers/isolated_container')
['default'];

... // test-helpers

window.exists = exists;
window.equal = equal;
window.strictEqual = strictEqual;
```

First, the `ember-testing-container` and `ember-testing` divs are injected into our test runner HTML page. The,n `Ember.testing` is set to true, which turns off the run-loop's autorun. Later you will see it is necessary to wrap any asynchrounous code within your tests with a `Ember.run()`, or you will receive the following message in your console:

```
You have turned on testing mode, which disabled the run-loop's autorun.
You will need to wrap any code with asynchronous side-effects in an Ember.run
```

Then, two additional boilerplate files are included and referenced globally through the window object.

As you might have noticed, the boilerplate has also included a number of test helpers that essentially just wrap QUnit assertions to use within your tests. Then, *test_helper.js* sets up global references to these helpers as well:

```
function exists(selector) {
  return !!find(selector).length;
}

function getAssertionMessage(actual, expected, message) {
```

```
    return message || QUnit.jsDump.parse(expected) + " expected but was "
      + QUnit.jsDump.parse(actual);
}

function equal(actual, expected, message) {
  message = getAssertionMessage(actual, expected, message);
  QUnit.equal.call(this, actual, expected, message);
}

function strictEqual(actual, expected, message) {
  message = getAssertionMessage(actual, expected, message);
  QUnit.strictEqual.call(this, actual, expected, message);
}
```

Then in *start_app.js*, EAK begins to initialize the application for the testing context. The `startApp()` method uses the imported app to create an instance of itself with configurable attributes, calls `setupForTesting()` (which defers the execution of application code), and injects the aforementioned test helpers:

```
import Application from 'appkit/app';

function startApp(attrs) {
  var App;

  var attributes = Ember.merge({
    // useful Test defaults
    rootElement: '#ember-testing',
    LOG_ACTIVE_GENERATION:false,
    LOG_VIEW_LOOKUPS: false
  }, attrs); // but you can override;

  Ember.run(function(){
    App = Application.create(attributes);
    App.setupForTesting();
    App.injectTestHelpers();
  });

  return App;
}

export default startApp;
```

The last file that is included to finish off the boilerplate for testing is called *isolated-Container.js*.

The purpose of this file is just what the name suggests, to provide an isolated copy of the `Ember.Container` for testing:

```
import Resolver from 'resolver';

function isolatedContainer(fullNames) {
  var container = new Ember.Container();
```

```
    container.optionsForType('component', { singleton: false });
    container.optionsForType('view', { singleton: false });
    container.optionsForType('template', { instantiate: false });
    container.optionsForType('helper', { instantiate: false });

    var resolver = Resolver['default'].create();

    resolver.namespace = {
      modulePrefix: 'appkit'
    };

    for (var i = fullNames.length; i > 0; i--) {
      var fullName = fullNames[i - 1];
      container.register(fullName, resolver.resolve(fullName));
    }

    return container;
  }

  export default isolatedContainer;
```

 In later versions of EAK, this functionality has been moved to the Ember-Qunit library. So if you are wondering where *isolatedContainer.js* is, you are probably running a later version of EAK. It will now be managed by bower and located in *vendor/ember-qunit/lib/*.

For more on Ember-Qunit, stay tuned—we will go into detail later in this chapter.

# Testem and QUnit Test Runners

EAK (Ember App Kit) ships with the Testem test runner (*https://github.com/airpor tyh/testem*) enabled by default. So for the beginning part of this chapter, we will be using this fantastic test runner.

Ember-testing uses QUnit, so one benefit to that is that we get the Qunit test runner that can run in the browser. When used with a test runner like Testem, we can also view our tests at the command line.

If we follow the standard *red-green-refactor* cycle of TDD (test-driven development), *broken* tests will display highlighted. It is your choice to monitor the tests at the command line or in the browser. Here is how your tests will look as you run them.

We can view our tests in a broken state first. Just open a terminal, navigate to the application directory, and run the test server:

```
$ cd rocknrollcall-eak

$ grunt test:server
```

You should then see the Testem test runner fire up and start executing our tests, as shown in Figure 10-1.

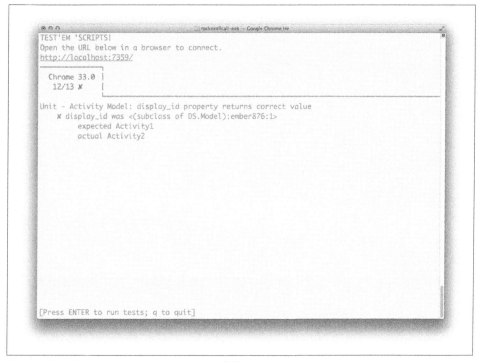

*Figure 10-1. Testem test runner: one test failing*

It is not the intention of this chapter to walk through the red-green-refactor cycle of each test, but by the end of this section, we should have a test suite of 13 passing unit and integration tests.

Again, open a terminal, navigate to the application directory, and run the test server, as shown in Figure 10-2:

```
$ cd rocknrollcall-eak
```

```
$ grunt test:server
```

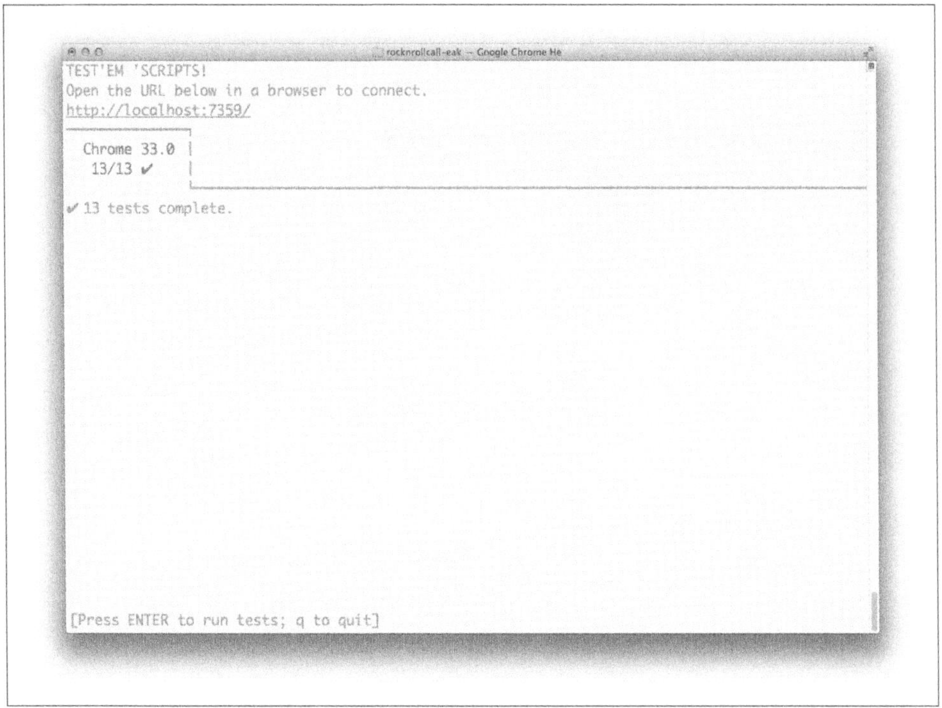

```
000                    rocknrollcall-eak — Google Chrome He
TEST'EM 'SCRIPTS!
Open the URL below in a browser to connect.
http://localhost:7359/

    ┌──────────────────┐
    │ Chrome 33.0 │
    │   13/13 ✔   │
    └──────────────┴──────────────────────────────
✔ 13 tests complete.



















[Press ENTER to run tests; q to quit]
```

*Figure 10-2. Testem test runner: all tests passing*

As mentioned, if you are not comfortable with running tests in the Terminal, you can also open a browser window to view your tests in the Qunit test runner and enter *http://localhost:7359/743/tmp/result/tests/index.html* (see Figure 10-3).

Now that we understand the basic setup, the Testem command line test runner, and the Qunit browser-based alternative, let's begin creating our first tests.

# Ember Client-Side Integration Testing

Let's begin with browser-only integration tests, perhaps one of the coolest aspects of the Ember framework. Here we can write and automate tests that exercise most of our application layers (router, models, controllers, and views) without the overhead of an application server, calls over the network, or even a database.

*Figure 10-3. QUnit test runner as an alternative*

## Helpers

The Ember testing module provides six helpers that automate interactions with your Ember application. These helpers include: `visit()`, `find()`, `fillIn()`, `click()`, `trig gerEvent()`, and `keyEvent()`.

There are also three helpers that return helpful information about the state of the application: `currentPath()`, `currentRouteName()`, and `currentURL()`.

For more information, see the Ember Integration Testing helpers section (*http://emberjs.com/guides/testing/integration/#toc_helpers*).

## Testing the Index Page

As mentioned earlier in the chapter, our testing setup also includes helpers that wrap QUnit assertions. To begin, we will do some `finds()` and use the `equal()` assertion that was explained earlier.

In *tests/acceptance*, we are given an *index-test.js* for free, as an initial example. In this example, we will do a basic setup and teardown of the application, and then run one test:

```
var App;

module('Acceptances - Index', {
  setup: function(){
    App = startApp();
```

```
    },
    teardown: function() {
      Ember.run(App, 'destroy');
    }
  });

  test('index renders', function(){
    expect(3);

    visit('/').then(function(){
      var title = find('h2#title');
      var list = find('ul li');

      equal(title.text(), 'Welcome to Ember.js');

      equal(list.length, 3);
      equal(list.text(), 'redyellowblue');
    });
  });
```

To break down this code further, notice that a QUnit `test()` accepts a description, `index renders`, and a callback function that contains the test. Within the test, we will first let Qunit know how many assertions to expect within this test. Keep in mind, if the number of assertions run doesn't equal the number passed to `expect()`, the test will not pass.

Then, we can use the `visit()` helper to access the index page, and use `then()` to handle the promise that is returned. Then, we use find to query the page for a few elements and assign them to variables. We then pass those HTML elements stored in variables, title and list, as the first parameter in our `equal()` assertion helpers. The second parameter in the `equal()` assertion helper is the value that we expect.

Figure 10-4 shows the results of this test.

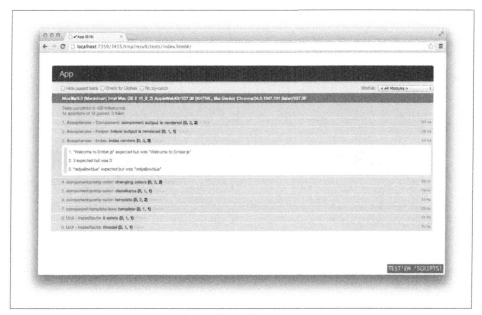

*Figure 10-4. Acceptance test: rendering the index page*

## Testing the Activities Route

In our next test, we will visit the `Activities` route, access the data model through Ember Data, and test that the data was properly displayed within the activities template.

In *tests/acceptance*, create an *activities-test.js* file:

```
var App;

module('Acceptances - Activities', {
  setup: function(){
    App = startApp();
  },
  teardown: function() {
    Ember.run(App, 'destroy');
  }
});

test('activities renders', function(){
  visit('/activities').then(function(){
    var title = find('h4');
    var list = find('ul li.activity');

    equal(title.text(), 'Total Activity Records: 2');
    equal(list.length, 2);
```

```
  });
});
```

See the change in this commit (*http://bit.ly/1nPKD8T*).

Our tests fail, as shown in Figure 10-5, but why?

*Figure 10-5. Acceptance activities fail: rendering the Activities page*

The answer is in the JavaScript error message that is being displayed in the browser console:

```
Failed to load resource: the server responded with a status of 404 (Not Found)
http://localhost:7359/api/activities
```

The reason we get this error is that our Ember application, actually Ember Data, is making a request to */api/activities* at the same domain as the Testem test environment, running on localhost, port 7359. The data is not available, because the Express app that serves the data is not running there.

To solve this issue, we need to make some minor configuration and code changes. This actually demonstrates more of Ember App Kit's extensibility and flexibility, a testament to the amount of thought put into how it was built.

First, we can create a host property in our test environment's config file:

```
window.ENV.host = 'http://localhost:8000'
```

And then use that property in *app/adapters/application.js* to tell Ember Data to point to the Express server running on the default port, which is different than our test environment:

```
export default DS.RESTAdapter.extend({
  namespace: 'api',
  host: window.ENV.host
});
```

This means we will need to run our Express.js app in a separate terminal:

```
$ grunt server
Running "expressServer:debug" (expressServer) task
Using API Stub
>> Started development server on port 8000.
```

and our test server in another:

```
$ grunt test:server

TEST'EM 'SCRIPTS!
Open the URL below in a browser to connect.
http://localhost:7359/
```

Almost there! Now, you should see an error in our browser's JavaScript console:

```
XMLHttpRequest cannot load http://localhost:8000/api/activities.
No 'Access-Control-Allow-Origin' header is present on the requested
resource. Origin 'http://localhost:7359' is therefore not allowed access.
```

This is an issue caused by trying to make a XMLHttpRequest to another domain. Fortunately, we can use node's `cors` `module` middleware to make this request return without error. The `cors` `module` utilizes the CORS specification to properly configure the Express server to handle cross-site XMLHttpRequests by adding a custom header to the response.

To enable CORS, we first add the new development dependency to our *package.json*:

```
"devDependencies": {
  "express": "~3.4.8",

  ...

  "cors": "2.2.0"
}
```

Then, add the `require` of the dependency in *tasks/express-server.js*:

```
var express = require('express'),
    lockFile = require('lockfile'),
    Helpers = require('./helpers'),
    fs = require('fs'),
    path = require('path'),
```

```
    request = require('request'),
    cors = require('cors');
```

And then add the middleware, just before the conditional logic that handles the prox
yMethod:

```
app.use(cors());

if (proxyMethod === 'stub') {
  grunt.log.writeln('Using API Stub');
  ...
```

And finally, we need to install the new dependency by running:

```
$ npm install
```

### More on CORS

CORS stands for cross-origin resource sharing, which is a specification that allows applications to make requests to other domains
from within the browser. With CORS, you have a secure and easy-
to-implement approach for circumventing the browser's same ori-
gin policy.

If you want another example using CORS, you can read about it in
more detail in Jesse Cravens and Jeff Burtoft's *HTML5 Hacks*
(O'Reilly, 2012); in particular, see Hack #75: Configure Amazon S3
for Cross-Origin Resource Sharing to Host a Web Font.

And now, we should see that our test environment is able to access the data from the
Express server and the test passes (Figure 10-6).

See these changes in this commit (*http://bit.ly/1nPLDK8*).

# Ember Unit Testing

Our first unit tests will test the existence of the Activities route, and exercise its
model method.

In unit testing a route, we immediately run into a few questions around how we
should manage data in our unit tests. If you are following along, you know that we
decided to make server-side fixtures on our Express server for our integration tests.

*Figure 10-6. Acceptance activities pass: rendering the Activities page*

EAK ships with a simple example of unit testing a route's `model` hook, but you may notice that the data is hardcoded or "mocked" as a returned array of values:

```
export default Ember.Route.extend({
  model: function() {
    return ['red', 'yellow', 'blue'];
  }
});
```

But what happens when our route actually calls the Ember Data store, such as our model hook in the `Activities` route:

```
export default Ember.Route.extend({
  model: function() {
    return this.get('store').find('activity');
  }
});
```

A number of things are different when we return data from Ember Data. The `model` hook is no longer isolated to the return of an array of values; the code now "calls out" to Ember Data's `find()`, and context travels through the implementation, resulting in a return of a promise. Because a promise is returned, the value from this hook needs to be resolved and handled differently than a simple return of an array of values. In other words, this `model` method invocation has now become an asynchronous operation.

This creates a number of questions about our testing strategy.

First, do we want to use the FixtureAdapter or the RESTAdapter to obtain the data? Or, do we want to isolate this functionality to a manually created mock object, therefore removing any interaction with Ember Data Adapters?

The answer lies in what we are intending to test, what we will be testing in our other tests such as our full-stack, integration tests, and possibly even our automated system tests. This is one area where the testing strategy debate can turn religious.

In general, our unit tests should maintain their own consistent test data to execute against. One reason this is important is so that the tests are portable and repeatable in different environments.

The other reason is so that the functionality we are testing is isolated to the unit we are testing and not impacted by another layer like the network or a database.

Where this is arguable, in an application of this kind, is at what level those fixtures are acceptable as isolated. If you are following along, you know we currently have fixture data *hardcoded* on the server in our Express app. You also know that, through the power of Ember Data, we have the ability to switch adapters and use the FixtureAdapter, essentially eliminating the network roundtrip.

For the sake of this tutorial, we will assume that our server-side fixtures are acceptable for our integration tests and for our unit tests, we will manage the data within client-side fixtures.

## Using Ember-Qunit

One reason why Ember-Qunit is important is that it provides for some of the setup boilerplate that used to have to be done manually.

Ember-Qunit provides three helpers: `moduleFor()`, `moduleForComponent()`, and `moduleForModel()`.

Perhaps the best way to understand the benfit of Ember-Qunit is by looking at the way we had to write our test setup module before we had `moduleFor()`:

```
module('Unit - ActivitiesRoute', {
  setup: function() {
    var container = isolatedContainer([
      'route:activities'
    ]);
    route = container.lookup('route:activities');
  }
});
```

In the past, you can see that we had to create a new `isolatedContainer` and then look up the route directly on the container. Now the functionality has been abstracted out to the `moduleFor()` wrapper. The same setup is now much less verbose:

```
moduleFor('route:activities', "Unit - ActivitiesRoute");
```

It still works in a similar way, but the lookup and management of the isolated container happens "behind the scenes."

The creation of the object we are testing is now returned by the `subject()` method. So we can then get access to the `ActivitiesRoute` within our test like so:

```
import Activities from 'appkit/routes/activities';

test("it exists", function(){
  ok(this.subject() instanceof Activities);
});
```

That's the basic idea, and we will dig into Ember-Qunit's other two helpers, `module ForComponent()` and `moduleForModel()`, in the following sections.

## Unit Testing Routes

So now that we understand that our setup has been simplified by Ember-Qunit, let's dissect the rest of the code. In *tests/unit/routes/activities-test.js*, we need to import the `test` and `moduleFor` functions from the Ember-Qunit module and the `Activities` Route. Then, pass `moduleFor()` the object to lookup, in this case the `activities:route`, and then we can give our test a meaningful description like quot;Unit - ActivitiesRoutequot;:

```
import { test, moduleFor } from 'ember-qunit';
import Activities from 'appkit/routes/activities';

moduleFor('route:activities', "Unit - ActivitiesRoute");
```

Then, our first two tests will assert the existence of the route from within the container, and that it as an instance of the `ActivitiesRoute`:

```
test("it exists", function(){
  ok(this.subject());
  ok(this.subject() instanceof Activities);
});
```

See the change in this commit (*http://bit.ly/1nPLXJ5*).

Looking good so far. Then, we will isolate the route's `model` hook by creating a simple mock `store` and defining a `find()` method. Then we assign the store to the route's `store` property. `find()` simply returns an array of one data object that we have manually copied from the `Activity` model's FIXTURES:

```
test("#model", function(){

  var store = {
    find: function() {
      return [{
```

```
                id: 0,
                display_id: 'Activity1',
                type: 'song',
                display_name: 'On The Road Again',
                hotttnesss: 54,
                timestamp: 'Fri Dec 06 2013 01:05:53 GMT-0600 (CST)'
            }
        ];
    }
};

var route = this.subject();

route.set('store', store);

deepEqual(route.model(), [{
    id: 0,
    display_id: 'Activity1',
    type: 'song',
    display_name: 'On The Road Again',
    hotttnesss: 54,
    timestamp: 'Fri Dec 06 2013 01:05:53 GMT-0600 (CST)'
    }
]);

});
```

See the change in this commit (*http://bit.ly/1nPLYN9*).

## Using Fixtures

This is one area where a testing debate can get started if we aren't careful; but to finish
these simple tests, we want to clean things up a bit. A unit test by definition should
really keep our code as isolated as possible, so some developers may argue that the
previous example ensures that isolation. Others may argue that they don't want to
manage the same data in two separate locations. But we know that the model fixtures
are simple arrays maintained elsewhere in the app (in this case, we declare them in
the Activity model *appkit/models/activity.js*) so it makes sense to import the fixture
data and reuse it in our tests.

This is the example data from our fixtures:

```
var Activity = DS.Model.extend({
  display_id: DS.attr('string'),
  type: DS.attr('string'),
  display_name: DS.attr('string'),
  hotttnesss: DS.attr('number'),
  timestamp: DS.attr()
});

Activity.FIXTURES = [
```

```
    {
      id: 0,
      display_id: 'Activity1',
      type: 'song',
      display_name: 'On The Road Again',
      hotttnesss: 54,
      timestamp: 'Fri Dec 06 2013 01:05:53 GMT-0600 (CST)'
    },

    {
      id: 1,
      display_id: 'Activity2',
      type: 'artist',
      display_name: 'Willie Nelson',
      hotttnesss: 99,
      timestamp: 'Fri Dec 06 2013 01:05:53 GMT-0600 (CST)'
    }
];

export default Activity;
```

See the change in this commit (*http://bit.ly/1nPM5br*).

Now by importing this data we can begin to use the data. The FIXTURES object is nothing more than an array at this point, so it is safe to use within our route unit tests.

Also notice that we aren't making use of the Activity model class, in order to not introduce another layer of functionality into our isolated ActivityRouter unit tests:

```
import { test, moduleFor } from 'ember-qunit';

import Activities from 'appkit/routes/activities';
import Activity from 'appkit/models/activity';

moduleFor('route:activities', "Unit - ActivitiesRoute");

test("it exists", function(){
  ok(this.subject());
  ok(this.subject() instanceof Activities);
});

test("#model", function(){

  var store = {
    find: function() {
      return Activity.FIXTURES;
    }
  };

  var route = this.subject();
```

```
    route.set('store', store);

    deepEqual(route.model(), Activity.FIXTURES);

  });
```

See the change in this commit (*http://bit.ly/1nPMavE*).

## Unit Testing Models

Finally, it is time to set up and test our models. Start by creating a new directory for these tests called *tests/unit/models/*. Then, create *activity-test.js* and place it within this directory.

In our setup, we can make use of Ember-Qunit's `moduleForModel` method:

```
import { test, moduleForModel } from 'ember-qunit';
import Activity from 'appkit/models/activity';

moduleForModel('Activity', "Unit - Activity");
```

First, we can check the existence of the model:

```
test("it exists", function(){
  ok(this.subject() instanceof Activity);
});
```

Then we begin to check that the values of the `Activity` model properties are what we expect them to be. Notice that we continue to manage the data in one place within the model's definition file:

```
test('#properties', function() {

  var activity = this.subject(Activity.FIXTURES[0]);

  equal(activity.get('display_id'), 'Activity1');
  equal(activity.get('type'), 'song');
  equal(activity.get('display_name'), 'On The Road Again');
  equal(activity.get('hotttnesss'), 54);
  equal(activity.get('timestamp'), 'Fri Dec 06 2013 01:05:53 GMT-0600 (CST)');
});
```

See the change in this commit (*http://bit.ly/1nPMhqY*).

# Wrapping Things Up

In this chapter, we started out covering our goals to have a testing setup that was simple, fast, and that provided readable tests. Along the way, we set up a Testem test runner, used CORS to configure our app to be used in our integration tests, covered the basics of Ember-Qunit, isolated functionality in unit tests, and mocked out some data with client-side fixtures.

# Index

controllers
  adding action references, 87
  generating in Rails, 128
  serialization and, 88
  tasks handled by, 85
  transient variable local, 86
CORS (Cross-Origin Resource Sharing), 157
css (folder), 11
currentPath(), 153
currentRouteName(), 153
currentURL(), 153

# D

D3.js library, 141
data attribute, 97
data binding, 15
data persistence
  abstraction layers
    Data Store, 109
    FixtureAdapter, 111
    LocalStorageAdapter, 111
    Serializer, 110
  basic client-side memory example, 100
  client-side libraries
    EBF (Ember Persistence Foundation),
      103
    Ember Data, 102
    Ember Model, 102
    Ember RESTless, 103
  Ember Data
    models, 104
    Router setup, 103
    tasks handled by, 103
    user interaction-based persistence, 106
debugging
  Activities Route, 157
  benefits of MVC design for, 6
  routes in the console, 70
  with Ember Inspector, 38
deleteRecord() method, 109
developer ergonomics, 8
developer workflow (see workflow management)
DS.Store, 109
dynamic routes, 75
dynamic segments, 76

# E

{{each}} helper, 56

EBF (Ember Persistence Foundation), 103
Echo Nest (music intelligence service), 46, 83
{{else}} helper, 58
Ember App Kit (EAK)
  overview of, 24
  testing with, 148
  unit testing with, 158
  with Express.js, 118
Ember backends
  protocols in use, 117
  RESTful Web Service APIs
    Ember App Kit (EAK) with Express.js,
      118
    Ember Data RESTAdapter, 118
  Ruby on Rails
    adding Ember, 130
    benefits of, 123
    Gemfile updates, 125
    generating initial application, 124
    installing, 124
    MVC/SPA, 127
    running tests, 129
    RVM (Ruby Version Manager), 123
    TurboLinks removal, 126
Ember components
  D3.js library, 141
  extending Ember.Component, 140
  template creation, 138
Ember Data
  models, 104
  overview of, 102
  RESTAdapter, 118
  Router setup, 103
  tasks handled by, 103
  user interaction-based persistence, 106
Ember Data Adapters, 117
Ember Data Store, 109
Ember Generator
  installing, 28
  installing dependencies, 27
  overview of, 23, 27
  running, 29
Ember Inspector, 38
Ember Model, 102
Ember object
  assigning properties to, 90
  creating, 100
Ember Rails
  active model serializer and, 132

model.save(), 109
models, in Ember Data, 104
modularized design pattern, 33, 103
moduleFor(), 160
moduleForComponent(), 160
moduleForModel(), 160
moment-to-moment state, 85
MVC (model-view-controller) architecture, 127

**N**

nicknames attribute, 58
Node.js, 9, 118
normalize.css, 11

**O**

Object class, 78
object relational mapper (ORM), 8
object-oriented programming (OOP), 5

**P**

pages, 67
Promises, 80, 90-97, 102
public/index.html, 127
Python
    downloading/installing, 14
    starting, 14

**Q**

QUnit, 150

**R**

RecordArray, 110
Red, Green, Refactor cycle, 150
rendering logic, 85
reopenClass, 101
require syntax, 32
resource not found (404) error, 156
RESTAdapter, 118
RESTful Web Service APIs, 118
RockNRollCall application
    feature overview, 45
    GitHub repo checkout, 25
    routers, routes and models for, 67
    template creation overview, 46
routers
    active generation and, 72
    benefits of, 67
    debugging routes in the console, 70

    declaring URLs in, 18
    default maps and routes, 71
    dynamic routes, 75
    matching model(s) with routes, 76
    Model classes and, 78
    model() method and, 81
    overview of, 17
    Promises feature and, 80
    routing in Ember.js, 69
    RSVP.js library, 81
    serialization and de-serialization, 68
RSVP.js library, 81
Ruby on Rails
    adding Ember, 130
    benefits of, 123
    checking for location of, 27
    development of, 9
    Gemfile updates, 125
    generating initial application, 124
    installing, 124
    MVC/SPA, 127
    removing public/index.html, 127
    running tests, 129
    RVM (Ruby Version Manager), 123
    TurboLinks removal, 126
RVM (Ruby Version Manager), 123

**S**

<script> tags, 50
separation of concerns, 33
serialization, 67, 88
Serializer, 110
.set(), 90
sets, 101
SimpleHTTPServer, 13
SPA (single-page application), 5, 127
SproutCore, 7
stubs, 118
style.css, 11

**T**

TDD (Test Driven Development), 150
templates
    {{action}} helper, 59
    bound attributes, 60
    custom helpers, 62
    {{each}} helper, 56
    for Ember components, 138
    for RocknRollCall application, 46

## About the Authors

**Jesse Cravens** is a principal web engineer at frog where he works with the world's leading companies, helping them to design, engineer, and bring to market meaningful products and services. He possesses a deep background in web application development, and has recently been focusing on single page web application architecture, the mobile web, and HTML5. Jesse's first book *HTML5 Hacks* (*http://html5hacks.com*) (O'Reilly, 2012) has been translated into multiple languages including Chinese and Japanese, and he has spoken internationally at conferences like SXSW Interactive, Fluent Conf, Future Insights, Code PaLOUsa, and Øredev.

He previously held senior development and technical management positions at USAA, leading a team of mobile application developers in the planning, designing, development, testing, implementation, and maintenance of USAA's industry leading iOS, Android, Blackberry, and mobile web applications for USAA's eight million members deployed worldwide.

Jesse holds a B.A. in Art from Rice University and a Master's degree in Curriculum and Instruction from the University of Texas at San Antonio.

You can find Jesse on the web at *http://jessecravens.com* or Twitter at @jdcravens.

**Thomas Q Brady** started, as so many did, with a Commodore computer as a child (Vic 20, though, not 64). At a very young age, he taught himself BASIC from the book that accompanied his computer, taking an odd route from there to Visual Basic to all-languages-web in a series of hobbies that, despite getting a degree in psychology and philosophy, became a career. Thomas has developed native desktop and mobile applications and web applications for clients from Harvard Business School Publishing to Disney to Standard and Poor's.

Since March 2014, Thomas has served as technology director at Reaction, Inc.

Thomas blogs at Bash Modern Quantity (*http://bashmodernquantity.com*) and tweets as @thomasqbrady.

## Colophon

The animal on the cover of *Building Web Apps with Ember.js* is a wood dormouse (*Muscardinus avellanarius*), which is native to northern Europe and Asia Minor and usually found in deciduous woodland and thick hedgerows. It is the only dormouse native to the British Isles, and is therefore often referred to simply as the "dormouse" in British sources.

Dormice can easily be recognized by their thick furry tail, bright golden-brown color, and large black eyes. They are about 70 millimeters long with a tail of similar length.

They are nocturnal creatures and spend most of their waking hours among the branches of trees looking for food: they eat berries and nuts and other fruit, with hazelnuts being the main food for fattening up before hibernation.

The old English name for the animal is "the sleeper" because dormice usually start hibernating at the first frosts, often in October and November, and are not active again until April or May. The hibernation nest is built on or near the ground, and the animal curls into a ball and goes to sleep. Their body temperature drops to that of the surroundings, and the heart and breathing rate are often reduced by 90% or more.

The main cause of the major decline of the dormouse over the last 100 years is the loss and fragmentation of its woodland habitat and changes in woodland management practices. Dormice are strictly protected by law and may not be collected, sold, or disturbed in any way.

Many of the animals on O'Reilly covers are endangered; all of them are important to the world. To learn more about how you can help, go to animals.oreilly.com.

The cover image is from Shaw's Zoology. The cover fonts are URW Typewriter and Guardian Sans. The text font is Adobe Minion Pro; the heading font is Adobe Myriad Condensed; and the code font is Dalton Maag's Ubuntu Mono.

# Have it your way.

# Get even more for your money.

## Join the O'Reilly Community, and register the O'Reilly books you own. It's free, and you'll get:

- $4.99 ebook upgrade offer
- 40% upgrade offer on O'Reilly print books
- Membership discounts on books and events
- Free lifetime updates to ebooks and videos
- Multiple ebook formats, DRM FREE
- Participation in the O'Reilly community
- Newsletters
- Account management
- 100% Satisfaction Guarantee

### Signing up is easy:

1. Go to: oreilly.com/go/register
2. Create an O'Reilly login.
3. Provide your address.
4. Register your books.

Note: English-language books only

**To order books online:**
oreilly.com/store

**For questions about products or an order:**
orders@oreilly.com

**To sign up to get topic-specific email announcements and/or news about upcoming books, conferences, special offers, and new technologies:**
elists@oreilly.com

**For technical questions about book content:**
booktech@oreilly.com

**To submit new book proposals to our editors:**
proposals@oreilly.com

**O'Reilly books are available in multiple DRM-free ebook formats. For more information:**
oreilly.com/ebooks

CPSIA information can be obtained at www.ICGtesting.com
Printed in the USA
BVOW09s0547140714

358699BV00002B/2/P

9 781449 370923